AROUND los angeles WITH KIDS

2nd Edition

by Lisa Oppenheimer

Fodor's Travel Publications
New York • Toronto • London • Sydney • Auckland

www.fodors.com

CREDITS

Writer: Lisa Oppenheimer
Series Editors: Karen Cure, Andrea Lehman
Editor: Andrea Lehman
Editorial Production: Taryn Luciani
Production/Manufacturing: Angela L. McLean

Design: Fabrizio La Rocca, *creative director;*
Tigist Getachew, *art director*

Illustration and Series Design: Rico Lins, Keren Ora
Admoni/Rico Lins Studio

ABOUT THE WRITER

Lisa Oppenheimer, mother of two, is a contributor to
Disney, Parents, and *Family Life* magazines as well as family travel columnist for Fodors.com. Lisa is also the author
of *Fodor's Around Boston with Kids.*

FODOR'S AROUND LOS ANGELES WITH KIDS

ISBN 0-679-00914-0
ISSN 1526-1387
Second Edition

IMPORTANT TIPS

Although all prices, opening times, and other details in this
book are based on information supplied to us at press time,
changes occur all the time in the travel world, and Fodor's
cannot accept responsibility for facts that become outdated or for inadvertent errors or omissions. So always confirm
information when it matters, especially if you're making a
detour to visit a specific place.

SPECIAL SALES

Fodor's Travel Publications are available at special discounts for bulk purchases for sales promotions or premiums. Special editions, including personalized covers,
excerpts of existing guides, and corporate imprints, can be
created in large quantities for special needs. For more information, contact your local bookseller or Special Markets,
Fodor's Travel Publications, 280 Park Avenue, New York, NY
10017. Inquiries from Canada should be directed to your
local Canadian bookseller or sent to Random House of
Canada, Ltd., Marketing Dept., 2775 Matheson Boulevard
East, Mississauga, Ontario L4W 4P7. Inquiries from the
United Kingdom should be sent to Fodor's Travel
Publications, 20 Vauxhall Bridge Road, London, England
SW1V 2SA.

PRINTED IN THE UNITED STATES OF AMERICA
10 9 8 7 6 5 4 3 2 1

COUNTDOWN TO GOOD TIMES

GET READY, GET SET!

Ask anybody about family attractions in Los Angeles, and chances are you'll get a lot of advice about going to Disneyland. It's good information, if not entirely accurate, since Disneyland is actually in Orange County. L.A. proper or no, Walt's original kingdom—or, more appropriately, kingdoms, now that Disney's California Adventure has moved in next door—is just one of scads of whiz-bang amusement meccas that have made Los Angeles and its neighboring counties a sort of theme park land. No fewer than five major theme parks coexist within the region. If that's not enough, drive a couple of hours south and you'll meet up with Legoland and SeaWorld, not to mention the San Diego Zoo and the Wild Animal Park.

WHAT TO DO

Still, there's more here than hair-rising rides. After all, though better known for fancy houses and fancier cars, L.A. has some pretty stellar natural scenery, too. One of the biggest bonuses of living here, in fact, is being able to take your pick of outdoor recreation, whether you prefer to be up to your ankles in hiking boots or up to your wetsuit in ocean. You can hang 10 one day and head for the hills the next, hiking on any of hundreds of trails in the Santa Monica Mountains (you'll find a few detailed here). Or bike one of the boardwalks along the coast.

Armchair sports lovers can pick from the well of L.A. teams. Count USC and UCLA among the colleges and the Anaheim Mighty Ducks, the L.A. Dodgers, and the mighty L.A. Lakers (if you're lucky, important, and/or wealthy enough to snag tickets) among the pros. Those who dream of stepping up to the mound can do the next best thing by taking a behind-the-scenes tour at Dodger Stadium (tel. 323/224–1400).

Not that you have to be a sports dude to love L.A. Cultural institutions are many—enough to fill a book all by themselves. Apart from those mentioned in the pages that follow, a few standouts include the Southwest Museum, the Japanese American Museum in Little Tokyo, and the Skirball Cultural Center. Art museums range from small, beach-side galleries, such as those in Laguna Beach, to sprawling compounds à la the Getty Center.

And, of course, there's "the Biz." Moviemaking in Hollywood isn't just a business; it's a way of life. Gobs of establishments are dedicated to the industry, including the Kodak Theater, the new home of the Oscar ceremonies. Organized tours run the gamut from the current homes of celebrities (Starline Tours of Hollywood) to the current homes of dead celebrities (Forest Lawn Cemetery) to the current homes of celebrities' dead pets (Los Angeles Pet Memorial Park).

If it's the production side you're interested in, you're in luck. Most local studios offer tours, and TV shows give audiences a firsthand look at a work in progress. You can also contact the L.A. Film Office (tel. 323/957–1000; www.eidc.com) to get a list of scheduled shoots.

RESOURCES

Even if you live in L.A., it pays to gather information like a tourist. A good place to start is one of the Visitor Information Centers (Downtown, tel. 213/689–8822; Hollywood, tel. 213/236–2331). You can also log on to www.lacvb.com.

HOW TO SAVE MONEY

We list only regular adult and child prices; children under the ages specified are free. It always pays to ask at the ticket booth whether any discounts are offered for a particular status or affiliation (but don't forget to bring your I.D). Many attractions offer family memberships, which often pay for themselves if you visit the attraction several times a year. If you like a place when you visit, you can sometimes apply the value of your one-day admission to a membership if you do it before you leave.

Look for coupons—everywhere from the local newspaper to a supermarket display to your pediatrician's office. Some places also offer frequent-visitor cards that give a free or discounted admission with a specified number of paid admissions. Also, keep an eye out for attractions— mostly museums and other cultural destinations—that offer free admission one day a month or one day a week after a certain time. We've noted several in this book.

More and more groups of attractions are offering combination tickets, which are cheaper than paying for admissions individually. Hollywood CityPass, for example, covers admission to Universal Studios, Autry Museum of Western Heritage, Hollywood Entertainment Museum, Museum of Television and Radio, Petersen Automotive Museum, Egyptian Theatre, and Starline Tours of Hollywood for about half the cost of separate entry. Purchase CityPass at one of the attractions or online (www.citypass.net), but you must use it within 30 days.

WHEN TO GO AND HOW TO GET THERE

With the exception of seasonal attractions, kid-oriented destinations are generally busiest when children are out of school—especially weekends, holidays, and summer—but not necessarily. Attractions that draw school trips can be swamped on a midweek morning. But such groups tend to leave by early afternoon, so weekdays after 2 can be excellent times to visit. For outdoor attractions, it's good to visit after a rain, since crowds tend to clear out. The hours listed in this book are an attraction's basic hours, not necessarily those applicable on holidays. It's always best to check.

Of course, you'll want to devise your travel schedule around Los Angeles's infamous rush hour, which actually spans roughly 6–9 in the morning and 3:30–6 in the afternoon. There's no perfect time to hit the road. Visitors always want to know when the traffic-free hours are; the unfortunate answer is "never." But peak-hour traffic jams, which can turn a 20-minute ride into an expedition worthy of rations and survival gear, should be avoided at all costs.

While your car remains by far the most efficient means of travel, public transportation—including Metro bus and rail (tel. 800/266-6883, www.mta.net) and the Dash buses (tel. 213/808-2273)—is getting better. And, with original art decorating some of the stations, mass transit can actually be a kick. (The MTA offers guided tours—by train, natch—of the stations.) Train travel is now possible along busy tourist routes, such as that connecting Universal City to Hollywood (red line) and downtown Los Angeles to Long Beach (blue line). The exact-change fare is $1.35 (25¢ extra for transfers); you can also buy cut-rate passes and discounted packages of tokens at Metro Customer Centers.

HOW TO USE THIS BOOK

Listed ahead are 68 of our picks for the best family spots the city and its neighbors have to offer. Info at the top details the staples: address, phone and Web site, hours, prices, and suggested ages. Look for other particulars—where to eat, nearby and related activities, and fun facts for kids—in the boxes. If you want to search for sights based on geography or subject matter, flip to the directories at the back of the book. And don't forget to create your own movie magic by looking in the bottom right corner while you flip the pages.

After you've explored a bit, let us know what you think. If you happened upon a place that you think warrants a mention, by all means, send it along. You can e-mail us at editors@fodors.com (specify Around Los Angeles with Kids on the subject line) or write to us at Around Los Angeles with Kids, Fodor's Travel Publications, 280 Park Avenue, New York, NY 10017. We'll put your ideas to good use. In the meantime, have fun!

Lisa Oppenheimer

ADVENTURE CITY

It's an age-old dilemma: your preschooler wants to go to theme parks, but the big parks have only a smattering of attractions that little ones can actually ride. This mini amusement park designed just for younger kids provides a solution. If your children jump for joy when the carnival trailers unfurl their awnings, they'll be in heaven in Adventure City, an upscale version of the familiar fairs on wheels you see setting up shop in the summer. Relative to the theme-park giants, kids enjoy the scaled-down rides, and parents appreciate the scaled-down prices. In fact, if you spend most of your time at the kiddie section of the bigger theme parks, you're much better off here.

The entire park is set up like a tiny town; there's a police station, train depot, and airport. Many of the 17 rides and attractions are of the spin-'til-you're-queasy variety that kids love. Fortunately, since you may be accompanying your children on some attractions, there are a number of non-stomach-churning rides to choose from, including a pint-size roller coaster and Ferris wheel, as well as a "crazy" school bus and a vintage miniature train driven

HEY, KIDS! There are a few things you should definitely not forget to do. Don't miss the tour of the police/fire station, where you can drive your own Adventure City emergency vehicle. And before you leave, remember to trade in your arcade winnings. Once outside the park, visit the mass of collectibles that is Hobby City, the original "City" that spawned the amusement park. If you're a doll fan, check out the Anaheim Doll & Toy Museum, in the White House, an impressive half-scale replica of that famous Washington home.

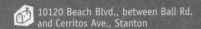 10120 Beach Blvd., between Ball Rd. and Cerritos Ave., Stanton

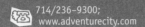 714/236-9300; www.adventurecity.com

 $11.95 ages 1 and up

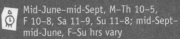 Mid-June–mid-Sept, M–Th 10–5, F 10–8, Sa 11–9, Su 11–8; mid-Sept–mid-June, F–Su hrs vary

 10 and under

by an affable engineer. One of the cutest of the lot is the Crank and Roll ride, where kids use their own steam to power a miniature train along a track. The park's full-size roller coaster, the Tree Top Racer, will placate older siblings, but it may be too wild for wee ones—even those who make the 42" height requirement. Other than rides, kids can choose from several fun activities. Animal lovers can visit with llamas, sheep, goats, rabbits, and chickens at the petting farm, while train enthusiasts can create their own track configurations at the vast Thomas the Tank Engine and Friends play area. There are live, interactive performances— puppet shows, sing-alongs, story times, and the like—held regularly at the outdoor theater, and your children can leave with painted faces and armloads of prizes from the park's arcade games.

Adventure City is also the perfect party place, with birthday packages available. But then every day's a party at this festive amusement park.

EATS FOR KIDS
Snack carts are spread around the park, but the only place with hot food is **Parker's.** Outside the park, try the aptly named **Restaurant Next to the White House** (Hobby City, 1238 S. Beach Blvd., Anaheim, tel. 714/827-0584), a little homespun breakfast and lunch spot.

KEEP IN MIND
Even though this isn't a mega-amusement park, plan on a trip here being a full-day event. Making that easier is Adventure City's pay-one-price admission, enabling your children to ride their favorites endlessly without repeatedly dipping into your pockets. Of course, any money you feel like you've saved can easily be dropped on arcade games and souvenir shops spread throughout the park.

ADVENTURE PLAYGROUND

This is the place to get down and dirty. A small slice of kid heaven in the middle of larger Huntington Central Park, Adventure Playground nevertheless packs much into its roughly ¾-acre confines, with mud, slides, tire swings, and a lot of appealing rough-and-tumble activity.

Your children will first encounter a small, manmade pond, where budding Huck Finns use mini-rafts and stick poles to get from one side to the other. Alongside, kids fly along on a tire attached to an overhead zip-line. Behind the pond sits the beloved mud slide and its grand finale: a splash landing in a delightfully muddy puddle.

But the most original part of the park—certainly the most memorable—is in back. At what amounts to a life-size erector set, your children can saw, hammer, and nail away, building actual structures they can then play inside. Staff members provide the building materials (two-by-fours, slabs of plywood, and even old tires) and tools (small hammers, dull

HEY, KIDS!

The mud slide is open sporadically during the day so make sure to be around for at least a few runs. When it's closed, head to the construction area. Though you can add to an existing structure, don't be shy about starting something new. At the end you'll be able to say, "I built it myself!"

KEEP IN MIND Adventure Playground's downscale charm can keep kids occupied for a whole day. Surprisingly, however, weekdays tend to be the most crowded, because the park is popular among camp groups; to avoid the rush, visit on a Saturday. Your children should wear sneakers that you don't mind getting trashed, as they are required in all park areas, including the water (no sandals allowed). Outdoor showers are available for post-mud rinsing. Children under 5 are admitted but cannot swim without a parent in the water. Reservations are recommended for groups of 10 or more.

 Huntington Central Park off Talbert Ave., Huntington Beach

 714/842-7442 (in season only)

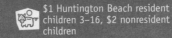 $1 Huntington Beach resident children 3–16, $2 nonresident children

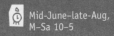 Mid-June–late-Aug, M–Sa 10–5

 5–12

saws); kids provide the imagination. Some add on to preconstructed tree houses; others start from scratch. The result is an amalgam of creative play spaces from wooden mazes to tepees to race cars. Sound structures are left standing until the park closes for the season at summer's end. Budding architects have been known to spend an entire day in the construction site. Adventure Playground has a small but extremely congenial staff of teens (plus an adult administrator) to lend a hand, but parents are expected to be the primary supervisors.

According to park operators, you needn't be skittish about either the neighboring Chevron holding station—admittedly an eyesore—or the park "dirt." Though the water looks murky, it's actually quite clean thanks to a cement bottom and regular water changing. And as for your children and their clothes, well, it should all come out in the wash.

EATS FOR KIDS Located inside Huntington Central Park, the **Park Bench** (17732 Golden West St., tel. 714/842–0775) serves breakfast and lunch daily. **Norm's** (16572 Beach Blvd., tel. 714/841–1919) serves a typically enormous 24-hour chain-restaurant menu.

AQUARIUM OF THE PACIFIC IN LONG BEACH

So, your kids think taking care of the goldfish bowl is a challenge? Try keeping up with a million-gallon aquarium. That unthinkable task is one of the things you'll learn about during the behind-the-scenes tour, the latest offering at this splashy and colorful aquarium on the shores of Long Beach. Opened in 1998, this ode to creatures of the Pacific ably pulls off its dual role as entertainer and educator. And you can get as close as possible to countless sea creatures—everything from playful puffins and Japanese spider crabs to rock fish and a 6-foot sea bass—without having to don wet suits.

Designers have worked hard to get you nose-to-gill with the scaly inhabitants (more than 12,000 animals in all), particularly in the Plexiglas tunnel aquariums, where water and fish surround you on all sides but beneath. The effect is particularly enthralling in the Tropical Pacific's Coral Tunnel, where colorful tropical fish seem to envelop you. (The exhibit is actually designed after a popular tropical reef off the island of Palau, in Micronesia.) The scuba feeling is enhanced further by the appearance of real divers, who

KEEP IN MIND Since its opening in 1998, the aquarium has proved extremely popular. Timed ticketing during busy times—particularly school vacations—cuts down the shoulder-to-shoulder experience. The rest of the year, try off-peak hours, roughly weekdays before 10 or after 2 or weekends by 9 or 10. Both should get you in the door line-free. The aquarium is closed one weekend each April (it changes year to year) for the Toyota Grand Prix through the streets of Long Beach; be sure to call ahead if you're planning a visit around that time.

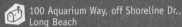
100 Aquarium Way, off Shoreline Dr.,
Long Beach

562/590-3100;
www.aquariumofpacific.org

$15.95 ages
12 and up, $8.95
children 3-11;
tour extra

Daily 9-6

All ages

submerge regularly to feed resident aquatic life and dispense fish facts (divers are outfitted with face-mask microphones that allow them to talk while they're submerged). Another popular spot is the outdoor seating area, where you can take a gander at perennial kids' favorites, such as harbor seals and sea lions.

For those who'd like to do more than just look, there are Discovery Labs for feeling the likes of sea urchins, crabs, and the snail-like sea hare. At the ever-popular skate and ray touch pools, your curious youngsters can reach out and touch the slippery stingray (stingers removed) and its relatives as well as a pair of leopard sharks. Small children can scurry about at Kid's Cove, pretending to be hermit crabs in the sand or walking through the "bones" of a giant gray whale skeleton. Be sure to meander through Kid's Cove's latest attraction: an aviary where you can actually feed the birds—not quite aquatic but quite fun.

EATS FOR KIDS
The aquarium's **Café Scuba** offers a food court–style selection of burgers, sandwiches, and snacks. Or grab the free shuttle to one of the downtown Long Beach eateries, including **Johnny Rockets** (245 Pine Ave., tel. 562/ 983–1332), a '50s-retro burger joint.

HEY, KIDS! While in the California Baja tunnels, see if you can get a sea lion to follow your finger. When they're in the right mood, the lively animals love to play along. But first, you'll have to get their attention, either with large movements or by waving a bright hat. In the Tropical Pacific area, look for leafy sea dragons. Related to sea horses, they're often hard to spot because they resemble weeds. Can you think why that would come in handy?

ATLANTIS PLAY CENTER

I f you're tired of the theme-park bustle (not to mention overstimulated kids), you'll find a welcome respite in this pleasing theme playground. Located in the larger Garden Grove Park, this much-loved playground is remarkable for its very ordinariness: one of those places you plan to go for an hour and wind up spending the entire day.

As the name suggests, the creative park is based on the famed lost city, although the ocean under which it's submerged must be invisible, as there is no water here save for a fountain or two. Spread inside a wooded 4-acre park are roughly 15 play sites, including sand-digging areas where climb-on sea creatures poke their heads out of the sand. Your children can zip down a whale slide and pop out through the orca's mouth or engage in all sorts of seafaring play around a beached Viking ship. The most beloved fixture here, by far, is the enormous Dragon Slide. Apart from kids' affinity for it, the slide rekindles a bit of nostalgia in parents,

HEY, KIDS!

No, this nifty little park has nothing to do with the Disney flick of the same name and actually predates the film by about 40 years. But both are children next to Atlantis itself. According to various versions of the legend, the island paradise existed more than 3,000 years ago.

KEEP IN MIND Sometimes, this play center can be the ideal, quiet setting; at others, the quiet is drowned out by noise. One source is a highway in close proximity to one of the park's boundaries, so be prepared for some traffic sounds. Another is the kids themselves. The park can get crowded with a capital "C," especially on Wednesdays and Thursdays, when the park often entertains school groups. And although the literature states "for ages 3–12," many parents feel it's more suited for those up to only 9 or 10.

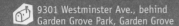 9301 Westminster Ave., behind
Garden Grove Park, Garden Grove

 $1 ages 2 and up

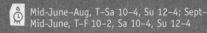 Mid-June–Aug, T–Sa 10–4, Su 12–4; Sept–
Mid-June, T–F 10–2, Sa 10–4, Su 12–4

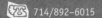 714/892–6015

 3–12

who can often be heard reminiscing about their own endless childhood slides down the thing. (The park has been a fixture since the 1960s.)

Though the equipment here makes this like other slightly revved-up playgrounds, what sets it apart is its setting. Atlantis is completely enclosed, with only one (attended) door through which you enter or exit. The added security allows you the luxury of enjoying a shady spot while giving your kids more freedom to play. Though you are still responsible for your children at all times, there are staff people on hand to keep the place in order. That means, among other things, that you'll get official reinforcement when you tell your youngster not to climb *up* the slide. And the fact that you have to pay to get in means that there's always somebody at the gate keeping adults from entering without a child and children from leaving without a parent.

EATS FOR KIDS Atlantis has lots of great picnic spots. If you forget to bring your own, have your hand stamped at the gate; you can then pick up eats at one of the numerous fast-food joints on Brookhurst Street and return. A **snack bar** operates in the park daily in summer and weekends the rest of the year. If you'd prefer something a little warmer, try **SouPlantation** (5939 W. Chapman Ave., tel. 714/895–1314), which serves a buffet of soup, salad, and pastas.

AUTRY MUSEUM OF WESTERN HERITAGE

64

The cowboy music playing in the plaza as you enter the museum is a tip-off to what's inside. Decades after Hollywood immortalized the American west via the Lone Ranger and Little Joe Cartwright, the Autry came along (in 1988) to give a real-life but fun look at this romanticized segment of American culture.

Kids will probably want to head straight to the lower level's Family Discovery Gallery. Formerly representing an Arizona ranch, the area was completely overhauled in 2001 and now depicts the life and times of a Chinese family originally lured west by the Gold Rush. Walk through Chinatown circa 1930, and find the F. Suie One Company, a store founded in 1888, and the Dragon's Den Restaurant. Still here are the interactive elements that made the original gallery a gem: the restaurant comes complete with role-playing tools (replica menus, waiter garb, and "food"), and the family home features board games, family letters, and scrapbooks.

KEEP IN MIND Though the facility bears the name of benefactor Gene Autry, don't expect a lot of exhibits dedicated to the famed movie cowboy. Mr. Autry, who died in 1998, mandated that the museum be used for American history, as opposed to Gene Autry history—hence the appearance of but one small showcase about the man himself. Before you come, ask about the museum's educational programs. The unusually creative and interesting special events include family festivals, ethnic arts and crafts, and storytelling. On some weekends, you can have souvenir photos taken in period garb.

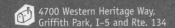
4700 Western Heritage Way,
Griffith Park, I–5 and Rte. 134

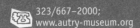
323/667–2000;
www.autry-museum.org

$7.50 adults, $5 youths
13–17, $3 children 2–12;
Th 4–8 free

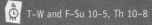
T–W and F–Su 10–5, Th 10–8

3 and up

Paraphernalia in other parts of the museum is equally sure to please. Life-size dioramas of the Old West include a full-size stagecoach, a saloon, and re-created scenes, such as the Earps and Clantons at the OK Corral. Kids can "lock up" their siblings in the authentically re-created jail (don't worry; the structure has only three sides) or ponder the weight of the cumbersome clothing ladies wore ("glittering misery," as these dresses were called). Upstairs you'll find a collection of western art as well as a tribute to western movie-making that contains a mosey-through street scene, famous film and television artifacts (look for the Lone Ranger's mask), and videos about western stunts. Despite its relatively small size, the outdoor Trails West exhibit does a nice job depicting the region's natural terrain, including rock formations, a pond, and a waterfall.

HEY, KIDS! You can't be in L.A. without a little movie magic. Climb on the saddle in the upstairs Spirit of Imagination gallery. The "horse" sits in front of a "blue screen," and through the magic of special effects, you can see yourself galloping along on the range.

EATS FOR KIDS The on-site **Golden Spur Cafe** is known for its shoot-'em-up homemade chili but serves burgers, hot dogs, sandwiches, and salads as well. The **Crocodile Café** (626 N. Central Ave., Glendale, tel. 818/241–1114) serves pastas, salads, sandwiches, and pizzas as well as a separate children's menu.

BUNNY MUSEUM

When owner Candace Frazee says you can't miss her quirky abode on a Pasadena side street, she isn't kidding. Home to this relatively new and oddly entertaining attraction, the one-story structure is earmarked with an 8-foot bunny on the front lawn.

The oversize lagomorph in question is late of Pasadena's fabled Rose Parade, one of thousands of long-eared statues, stuffed animals, and even live hoppers that Frazee and her husband Steve Lubanski have acquired over the years. Displayed inside are more than 12,000 bunnies of every shape, size, color, and creed.

The museum's collection, the world's largest according to the 1999 *Guinness Book of World Records,* sprouted from sentimentality. Early in their relationship, Lubanski gave his "honey bunny" a stuffed rabbit, and the rest is hare-story. The two have exchanged bunny presents every day since, resulting in bunny silverware, bunny dishes, bunny furniture, bunny toilet seat covers…well, you get the idea. The front room is filled with figurines;

KEEP IN MIND Reservations are required for admission, but once you're there, you can stay as long as you like. Reservations are not required on major holidays (such as Easter), when the Bunny Museum hosts open houses.

EATS FOR KIDS Hop over to **Pinocchio's Pizza** (1427 N. Lake Ave., tel. 626/791–7591), where locals swear by the divine, blissfully un–chain–like pies. If the kids are game to try something new and different, head for the superb Middle Eastern kebabs and more at the **Lebanese Kitchen** (1384 E. Washington Blvd., tel. 626/296–9010). **Acapulco Mexican Restaurant** (2060 E. Foothill Blvd., tel. 626/449–7273) serves enchiladas, salads, and maybe a little "hare" of the dog.

 1933 Jefferson Dr., Pasadena

 Free

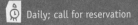 Daily; call for reservation

626/798-8848;
www.thebunnymuseum.com

 4–12

the den is loaded with stuffed bunnies. The backyard has original bunny art (granite benches) as well as a bunny garden (she grows only what bunnies eat) and a bunny-shaped fish pond— the beginnings of what Frazee envisions as an eventual bunny village.

Frazee gamely conducts tours of her abode, paws-ing before bunnies of honor to tell stories of their acquisition and to wax poetic about her dream of someday opening a BunnyLand theme park. Though the owners are strict about not touching most objects, they make the experience family-friendly by reading aloud from one of their 500 bunny children's books and by allowing youngsters to play with some toys, such as bunny bowling (with bunny pins) and bunny jump ropes. Frazee even encourages kids to get creative with the chalk she provides for the driveway.

While the place rates as a bit of an oddity, kids (and adults) seem to get a kick out of its general quirkiness. And where else can you see a bunny dressed up as Elvis?

HEY, KIDS! One of the most unusual bunny sculptures in the museum is fondly called Moo Doo. The "Moo" refers to the kind of animal that produced the ingredients for the sculpture. We'll let you guess what the "Doo" is. Zoo Doo, a sibling sculpture, was a joint effort among several animals living in captivity.

CABRILLO MARINE AQUARIUM

Think of this aquarium on the beach as more of a marine education center than a simple tourist attraction. And that is precisely the fun. Located on the San Pedro coast, this intimate facility is a place where families can not only look at tanks full of marine life, but also go out in the wild with the experts and explore.

A visit to the museum can be split into two parts. Inside, roughly 7,500 square feet of exhibit space contains 35 aquariums displaying southern California marine life. Some of the habitats include touch tanks, and many feature hands-on activities. The facility also houses a small research laboratory that doubles as an aquatic nursery, where such creatures as jelly fish are raised. The lab is open to the public; in fact, visitors are often invited to become involved in research projects (as researchers, not subjects!).

Though the interior tanks are indeed beautiful, outside is where the aquarium's individuality really shines. With harbor and ocean beaches right at its front door, the facility is equipped

KEEP IN MIND The aquarium runs several special programs that might interest your family, so it's a good idea to call before you come in order to find out what's happening when. Grunion programs occur twice monthly from March to July, but since they don't begin until 9 PM, they are better for older children. Tide-pool tours are given on most weekends, and though reservations are not required, you'll still want to call ahead to check on the schedule, which is dependent on low tide. During the winter, the aquarium runs two-hour whale-watching tours ($15) to see the migration of the California gray whales.

 3720 Stephen White Dr.,
San Pedro

 310/548-7562;
www.cabrilloaq.org

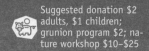 Suggested donation $2
adults, $1 children;
grunion program $2; na-
ture workshop $10–$25

 T–F 12–5, Sa–Su 10–5

 2 and up

for such natural explorations as tide pooling, which takes place most weekends. One of the most popular events is the annual grunion program. During spawning season (March to July), the small, native southern California grunion swims in to deposit its eggs in the sand; if you visit on a selected night during this time, you can join a staff-led foray to watch the spectacle of literally thousands of these silver fish surfing up to the shore. Normally, the eggs remain buried and unhatched until the tide washes them free. Occasionally, however, Cabrillo staff retrieve eggs that can be hatched in the lab by visitors who add sea water and a good shake.

You can also participate in one of the aquarium's nature workshops. Wednesday afternoons, look for free Marine Lab programs with games, crafts, and other activities aimed at aquatic education.

GETTING THERE Finding the aquarium can be tricky if you don't know where you're going. Take I–110 to the Harbor Boulevard exit; turn right on Harbor Boulevard and right again on 22nd Street. Then turn left on Pacific Avenue, and take it to Stephen White Drive.

EATS FOR KIDS The **Lighthouse Deli** (508 W. 39th St., tel. 310/548–3354) serves breakfast and lunch deli favorites. The friendly **Pacific Diner** (3821 S. Pacific Ave., tel. 310/831–5334) is presided over by owner Dennis Jewett and family, who serve up comfort-food favorites (meat loaf, pot roast) as well as some Mexican-inspired egg dishes for breakfast and lunch daily.

CALIFORNIA SCIENCE CENTER

The California Science Center is one of those facilities that seems to be routinely showing up on kids' "favorite" lists these days. Opened in 1998, this nifty place is no "look but don't touch" showroom, but rather a tinkerer's paradise where gizmos and gadgets bring to life many of those science principles your young students have been learning about in the classroom.

Most of the center's permanent exhibits are divided between two galleries: the World of Life and the Creative World. World of Life is where you can get a leg up on the living body—human, animal, or plant—through any number of activities. Your children can take a virtual tour through the human circulatory system via a red blood cell or watch the body's physiological changes via a multimedia presentation of Tess, the translucent 50-foot woman.

HEY, KIDS!

Ever think of art as a kind of science? Some of the greatest artistic achievers—Leonardo Da Vinci, for example—were also scientists. And someone had to come up with the formula for those crayons. Check out the Art & Science studio to explore the subject further.

KEEP IN MIND

All the neat toys here can make hours go by in what seems like moments, so plan to stay at least half a day. Head to the high-wire bicycle early, as the attraction usually has a line later on. For further explorations, ask about the institution's Science Workshops (extra charge), for kids pre-K to 10th grade. These weekend classes, held in rooms just outside the main facility, use science center–style approaches to learning such sciences as chemistry, physics, and biology.

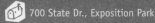 700 State Dr., Exposition Park

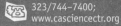 323/744-7400;
www.casciencectr.org

 Free; IMAX 3-D $7.50
adults, $6 students 13–17,
$4.75 children 4–12 (2-D
$1 less); bicycle $2

 Daily 10–5

 5 and up

The Creative World explores technology, and this is where your curious ones will find the real toys: digital wizardry that allows them to "morph" their own photographed image, a computerized musical jam session, and a video periscope that lets them chat with tourists in other areas of the building. And that's just the beginning. Each gallery also has a discovery room, where younger kids can conduct hands-on activities with Mom and Dad or see live animals, such as butterflies, frogs, mice, and snakes. The center also has a special-exhibits gallery, containing an ever-changing series of traveling exhibits.

Of course, a visit to the center wouldn't be complete without a ride on the high-wire bicycle, a display about the force of gravity masquerading as a circus act. Strung across a wire three stories up, the bicycle seems to defy gravity, allowing strapped-in riders to pedal back and forth without tipping over. (The feat is accomplished thanks to a weight on the bicycle's underside.) And don't miss the much-raved-about IMAX theater, where 3-D features are shown on a giant, seven-story screen.

EATS FOR KIDS The science center has a choice of three convenient places to eat: **Megabites Cafe,** which has pizza, salads, and a grill; the self-explanatory **McDonald's;** and the quiet **Rose Garden Cafe,** which serves coffee, dessert, and sandwiches (but usually not in that order) overlooking the historic rose garden. You can also sample the Korean-influenced fare at **Woo Lae Oak** (see the Los Angeles County Museum of Art).

CASA DE TORTUGA

You might call Casa de Tortuga (House of Turtles) a hobby that's gotten out of hand. What started with one man's fondness for a couple of turtles turned into a collection of hundreds of these green creatures, so many he had to build a separate structure to house them all.

Walter Allen's preoccupation with turtles has become a tourist treasure. A quirky animal habitat dedicated to the preservation of shelled creatures big and small, Casa de Tortuga is certainly a novel wonder in the world of animal attractions, if only for the surprise of finding out just how many different species of turtle actually exist—about 220 for anyone keeping a tally.

A tour literally takes you through Allen's backyard. On display are hundreds of specimens he's picked up through his world travels. Beyond just your aquarium-variety water turtles and box turtles (the two types commonly found at pet shops), there are also red-eared

HEY, KIDS! Make sure to tell your friends about the three Aldabra tortoises here, one of which was donated by Michael Jackson. The largest breed of tortoise, these giants can grow to be about 650 pounds and live to be a couple of hundred years old. Thinking about breeding your own family of Aldabras? That can be pretty complicated, since you can't tell the difference between the males and the females until they reach adulthood.

 Fountain Valley (call for precise address)

 M–Sa 10

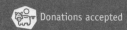 Donations accepted

 6 and up

714/962–0612

sliders, Burmese, Sulcatas, and Russian tortoises. Pieces of erroneous turtle lore are intriguingly dispelled along the way. Some turtles (desert turtles, for example) live nowhere near water, and anyone brought up on the "Tortoise and the Hare" legend will be shocked at the speed at which some of the big guys can travel.

Your children will no doubt be awed by the displays, especially by those of the giant species, which live in structures larger than a typical dog house. Be prepared for the inevitable exit question: "Mom, can I get a turtle?" Many kids, and parents, do leave with visions of turtles dancing in their heads. But Casa staff are quick to provide reality checks, such as the fact that all turtles need to be housed outside. Casa does provide "adoption" services to qualified individuals and helps kids understand the care and feeding of these guys through activity and coloring pages provided on the way out.

KEEP IN MIND Allen restricts tours to once daily, so as not to disturb the neighbors. Drop-ins are not accommodated; you'll get the address when you make reservations. Though small groups may get weekday reservations quickly, plan months ahead for a Saturday. And do not touch the turtles.

EATS FOR KIDS You may have to wait, but the **Rainforest Cafe** (3333 Bristol St., Costa Mesa, tel. 714/424–9200), with its Animatronic animals, talking trees, and large menu (but no turtle soup!), is a kick for kids. There are scads of eateries along nearby Brookhurst Street. Among them: **Applebee's Neighborhood Grill & Bar** (18279 Brookhurst St., tel. 714/963–1835) with its typical chain fare of fajitas, salads, and sandwiches.

CATALINA ISLAND

Half the fun of visiting this lovely island off the southern California coast is getting here. Modern boats make the scenic one-hour cruise from Long Beach (among other ports) a pleasure; if you're lucky, you might see a school of dolphins swimming by or, during the winter months, a pod of California gray whales on their annual migration.

Once you're on Catalina (officially Santa Catalina Island), you'll find it a world removed from the bustle of Los Angeles. Although your first glimpse upon landing is of the quaint and thriving seaport town of Avalon, roughly ¾ of this splendid adventure land is in its natural state, making it ideal for exploration.

First, decide on a mode of transportation. Cars are permitted here by permit only, so you'll have to leave yours at home. Options include bikes, golf carts, taxis, and—dare we suggest it!—even walking. Avalon, in fact, is laid out in particularly user-friendly fashion, making hoofing a delightful way to get around.

EATS FOR KIDS The **Busy Bee** (306 Crescent Ave., tel. 310/510–1983) serves salads, burgers, and such at umbrella tables overlooking the bay. **Antonio's** (114 Sumner Ave., tel. 310/510– 0060) is a funky place for pizza and pasta.

KEEP IN MIND Rent bikes from Brown's Bike (107 Pebbly Beach Rd., tel. 310/510–0986), golf carts from Cartopia Golf Cart Rentals (Crescent Ave. and Metropole St., tel. 310/510–2493), and horses from Catalina Stables (600 Avalon Canyon Rd., tel. 310/510–0478). Check out Catalina Discovery Tours (tel. 310/510–8687) or Adventure Tours (tel. 310/510–2888) for land, glass-bottom boat, or semisubmersible tours; Catalina Ocean Rafting (tel. 310/510–0211) for raft tours; and Descanso Beach Ocean Sports (tel. 310/510–1226) or Wet Spot Rentals (tel. 310/510–2229) for kayaks and kayak tours.

Catalina Island Visitors Bureau,
Box 217, Avalon 90704

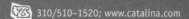 Free

310/510-1520; www.catalina.com

Boats usually 6:30-5, later June-Aug

 All ages

Strolling among Avalon's many shops and restaurants is an itinerary mainstay. Further land explorations can be made via one- to four-hour open-tram tours. Shorter jaunts give you a general lay of the land, whereas longer trips reveal some of the island's more unusual aspects, such as the thriving herd of bison, brought over by a film crew in the 1920s and left to roam free. You might also opt for a trip on horseback. A few operators offer ocean raft and kayak tours; in addition to paddling through caves and interesting coves, you may spy a bald eagle or two.

Undersea sights are plentiful as well. Catalina is well known as a haven for snorkelers and scuba divers, but bring a wet suit, as water is only temperate July–September. For underwater scenery without spoiling your good hair day, try either a glass-bottom boat or semisubmersible tour, both available at Lover's Cove.

GETTING THERE If you don't have your own helicopter or private yacht, you'll have to settle for public transport. Catalina Express (tel. 800/481-3470) has service ($39 adults, $29.50 children 3–11, $2 children 2 and under) from Long Beach and San Pedro; transportation from Dana Point is slightly more. Catalina Passenger Service (tel. 949/673-5245) runs from Newport Beach ($39 adults, $23 children 3–12, $2 children 2 and under). Fares quoted are round-trip, and reservations are a must.

CHILDREN'S MUSEUM AT LA HABRA

This comfortable and unassuming children's museum in a renovated 1923 train depot really lets kids go to town. Bright and cheery, the place has no shortage of things to do, and you may well end up having to drag your kids away from the action at the end of the day.

Though seemingly small from the outside, the museum seems to go on forever, with rooms extending out from either side of the entrance. Your children, however, may have trouble making it past the first room, where a Dino Dig pit is the perfect site for excavation and a gas station lets them "fill 'er up" just like a grown-up. In fact, the pump sports price and gallon meters that really run. Your youngsters will thank you for paying the electric bill after pedaling the foot-powered generator. The harder they pedal, the more bulbs they light, but lighting them all takes a *lot* of effort.

KEEP IN MIND If you want to have the museum all to yourself, plan to come during off hours. The quietest times are weekdays after 2, when school groups have gone home. Saturdays are almost always crowded, but often with good reason; the museum offers special events—storytelling, art workshops, and puppet theater—two or three Saturdays each month.

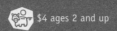

Other rooms feature a city bus (the front third of a real one), a well-stocked grocery store, an old-time switchboard, and a fully furnished dollhouse. Train enthusiasts can toot the whistle on the elaborate model train set; be sure to ask about tours of the antique caboose (outside in the train yard) that take place hourly. An indoor "nature walk" lets your children check out a beehive in operation and pet the fur of an impressive collection of taxidermic animals, including bears, elk, mountain lions, and a coyote.

Future movie stars can get ready for their close-up in the museum's impressive Kids on Stage section, featuring the largest dress-up area most children have ever seen, a piano, microphone, a glamorous stage, and a technical booth from which kids can operate the stage lights. Beyond that is the Preschool Playpark with a tree house for climbing, as well as sturdy plastic toys, including trucks and a play kitchen and tables. What else could a child possibly need?

EATS FOR KIDS **Marie Callender's** (340 Whittier Blvd., tel. 562/691–0705) serves the chain's dependable fare of family favorites: burgers, salads, pastas, and pizzas. The selection at **Applebee's Neighborhood Grill & Bar** (1238 W. Imperial Hwy., tel. 562/690–0779) isn't as vast, but the restaurant has tasty appetizers, salads, sandwiches, and entrées. Seasonal specialties give the menu spice.

CLAY CLUB

Sometimes you've just got to flex your creative muscles. When the mood hits, and your children want to create a ceramic masterpiece, head straight for Clay Club.

A paint-your-own pottery place, Clay Club has been on the Los Angeles scene for nearly a decade, offering children, parents, and often grandparents an outlet for their innermost artiste. Choose from one of more than 700 unpainted ceramic pieces, grab your brush, and go to work.

Available pieces range from mugs to dinnerware to character-ish figurines. Prices vary wildly, from a low of a few dollars for a small dog to a high of about $70 for an enormous floor vase. If price alone isn't enough to deter your little one from some of the loftier items, remind her (or him) that such complicated pieces can be difficult to paint. Items such as menorahs and Santa plates are on hand year-round, so you can start working

HEY, KIDS!
Stumped about where to begin? Clay Club has idea books that can stimulate your decorative side and get you going. Also ask about stencils and rubber stamps to add to the design.

KEEP IN MIND Clay Club has another location, in West L.A. (10522 Pico Blvd., Los Angeles, tel. 310/202–0888). The Woodland Hills location is a little more manageable, if only because it has readily available, free parking. Ask about discounted studio costs on Sunday afternoons. Finished pieces are safe to put food on and are dishwasher- and microwave-safe. Birthday parties can be held on-site, or you can have all the ingredients for a party brought to you.

 20929 Ventura Blvd., Woodland Hills

 Ceramic pieces from $5; studio time $7 ages 15 and up, $5 children 14 and under

 Daily 12–6

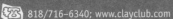 818/716–6340; www.clayclub.com

 6 and up

on holiday gifts early. Coming up on Mother's or Father's Day? Staff can help your children create their ceramic handprints.

Clay Club provides all the paint, brushes, and glaze you'll need. There's no additional charge for firing, but you'll have to come back and pick up the finished product the next day.

Colors are supposed to wash out of clothes, but you should probably wear old duds, and perhaps borrow one of the club's aprons. The water-based, nontoxic paints have the fringe benefit of being rinseable. That means little perfectionists can wash away mistakes before they dry (once paints set—you're stuck). Still, take your time, as even rinsed colors can leave a stain on the ceramic. There's no limit to how much time you can spend. If you have to leave before you finish, you can pay the studio fee again another day and finish up.

EATS FOR KIDS Family-friendly **Nicola's Kitchen** (20969 Ventura Blvd., tel. 818/883–9477) serves tasty, affordable Italian food—including pizza—with a California flair. **Cable's Restaurant** (20929 Ventura Blvd., tel. 818/347–2437) is the place for good coffee-shop fare.

DESCANSO GARDENS

When people call Los Angeles a jungle, they're not talking about serene, wooded Descanso, where you can stroll with your kids past fish-filled streams and paths planted with a pleasing collection of flowers and shrubs. A 20-minute drive north from downtown, near Pasadena, the gardens feel utterly insulated from the world outside. Bunnies, squirrels, and ducks scurry (or waddle) about, and koi swim in a tranquil lily pond with stone fish sculptures that spout water from puckered mouths.

No stuffy botanical garden—there's not a KEEP OFF THE GRASS sign in sight—Descanso positively encourages kids to run, not walk, the easy-to-maneuver paths that go uphill, around streams, and through a towering 35-acre oak forest—a rarity in southern California. You can also opt for a guided tram tour. The 160-acre site—vast enough for Walt Disney to have once considered it instead of Anaheim for his theme park—encompasses everything from a bird sanctuary to a Japanese tea garden.

KEEP IN MIND Something's always in bloom. Camellias bloom from September to April, tulips and other spring flowers in March and April, and roses from May to December. Descanso's busiest time is mid-March to mid-April, during the Spring Festival of Flowers. The event's special children's nature walks and activities—and the fact that the train runs daily—make this ideal for families; just come during the week or by 10 on weekends to avoid crowds. The popular winter holiday festival (with Santa) arrives in early December. All these events make a $60 family membership economical.

The genus and species of Descanso's multitude of blooms and shrubs probably won't bowl younger children over. "Look, Mommy, pretty flowers!" is about the best you can hope for. Some blooms, including the 5 acres of roses that come out each May, do seem to appeal to even the littlest visitors. But by and large, the bright colors and wide open spaces are the real attention grabbers, enough to make for happy—and tired—campers at the end of the day.

Descanso also has a few kid treats up its sleeve. The Secret Garden in the International Rosarium is a child-size retreat within a retreat, a charming little garden tucked inside a scaled-down hedge maze. Hedges are short enough for you to keep watch from outside. There's also the scale-model Enchanted Railroad (run only on weekends for much of the year), which your youngsters can ride on as it winds through parts of the forest. But it's really only one of many enchanted and enchanting attractions here.

HEY, KIDS! Those beautiful flowers in the oak forest, called camellias, are the reason Descanso exists. It started as a camellia nursery. Ordinarily about 8 feet tall, camellias grow to 35 feet here, due largely to their age. Some plants are 60 years old—even older than your parents!

EATS FOR KIDS Why not bring a picnic to these beautiful grounds? Alternatively, eat at the on-site **Cafe Court** (tel. 818/952–0219). Though the fare—sandwiches, salads, fruit—is standard, you can't beat the convenience and price. Coloring-book menus and balloons entertain kids at the diner-style **Hill Street Café** (1004 Foothill Blvd., tel. 818/952–1019), where friendly waiters bring tasty, reasonably priced meals: spaghetti, burgers, and corn dogs for kids, chicken, fish, and pasta for adults.

DISCOVERY MUSEUM OF ORANGE COUNTY

Most parents feel lucky if their kids remember to pick their clothes up off the floor, so many are utterly bemused to watch those same children become rapt in the task of washing towels on a turn-of-the-last-century washboard. But such is the fun at this historic Santa Ana museum, which features four antique Victorian structures where your children can tinker on long-defunct gadgets to learn about what life was like about a century ago.

Each room in the main building, the 100-plus-year-old Kellogg House (named after its original owner), represents a different theme, most with workable objects of the time. The most popular spot by far is upstairs in the Textile Room, where boys and girls can try on antique finery and learn about those funny-looking knickers and bonnets they'd be sporting if they'd been born just 10 or so decades before. Of course life wasn't all bad. A visit to the home's bathroom reveals that in the days before running bath water, tubs had to be painstakingly filled with water heated on the stove. The result was that people only took a bath once a week.

EATS FOR KIDS The museum has picnic areas. South Coast Plaza can satisfy everyone's tastes. **Back Bay Rowing and Running Club** (3333 Bristol St., tel. 714/641–0118) has fish, grills, and a salad bar. Across the street is the ever-dependable **Ruby's** (333 Bear St., Costa Mesa, tel. 714/662–7829).

HEY, KIDS! At the working Blacksmith's Shop, you can explore the blacksmith trade of a century ago. Pound an anvil, blow the bellows, or, if you're really lucky, watch the blacksmith of the day work on his latest project. (Blacksmithing demonstrations are guaranteed on the third Sunday of each month but often occur more frequently.) Today's blacksmiths still ply their trade making horseshoes and even repairing large equipment, such as bulldozers. Can you think of other things they might do?

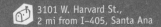 3101 W. Harvard St.,
2 mi from I–405, Santa Ana

 $5 ages 3 and up

 W–F 1–5, Su 11–3

714/540-0404;
www.discoverymuseumoc.org

 3 and up

There are (gasp!) no video games in the Children's Room, but kids seem amply entertained by the electronics-free toys of the time, such as a ticktacktoe board, pickup sticks, a dollhouse, and a sewing machine. Downstairs, the front parlor has a workable Victrola, Edison Talking Machine, pump organ, and hand-crank telephone. In the kitchen, look for, among other things, a butter churn and an old-fashioned stove-top toaster.

There's more activity outside. Spread around the museum's 12-acre property is a nature center, featuring reptiles, birds' nests, and habitat for other animals, as well as a small barnyard area with the usual petting-zoo suspects (sheep, goats, etc.). At the Eco-Art Gallery, kids can create masterpieces out of recycled materials (no extra charge). Visiting on a Sunday? Ask about special Sunday activities such as guided nature walks and crafts.

KEEP IN MIND The Discovery Museum's goal is to illustrate life in days of yore. With that in mind, many activities are of the gone-but-not-forgotten, quaint, and low-tech variety, such as Children's Teas, which are held on holidays such as Valentine's Day and Easter. The flagship event here is the annual 1890s Market Day, when period-clad actors, as well as participatory crafts, games, and contests, re-create a 19th-century celebration. Check the museum's September schedule for dates.

DISCOVERY SCIENCE CENTER

This is *not* where Pietro the Human Pincushion defies pain and agony while lying on a bed of nails. It's where you and your children will, discovering not only that it's not at all painful but also why. This science museum, opened in 1998, gets participants wholly involved in science by doing things like lying on that bed of nails, thus learning the secret of weight disbursement (and, thankfully, not of acupuncture) and why sitting on a thousand nails hurts so much less that sitting on just one.

Though "hands-on" has become the mantra of virtually all of today's interactive museums, the twist at the 59,000-square-foot Discovery Science Center is the number of so-called body-on activities, exhibits that allow your family to become immersed in the process of learning about science. In addition to lying on nails, you can experience earthquakes of varying intensities, walk through a tornado, and create your whole-body impression in a wall full of pins, the super-size version of those hand-held gizmos you find at toy stores.

GETTING THERE Finding your way to the science center seems easy, but there are a couple of tricky turns, particularly if you're coming from the north. If you're driving south on I–5, exit at Main Street North. Take your first left onto Santa Clara Avenue and the next left onto Main Street. The science center is on your left. From the south, head north on I–5, also exiting at Main Street North. Turn right off of the ramp onto Main Street. Then take your first left into the parking lot. Keep an eye out for the center's hallmark 10-story cube.

 2500 N. Main St., Santa Ana

 714/542–2823;
www.discoverycube.org

 $9.50 adults,
$7.50 children 3–17;
3-D laser show $1

 Daily 10–5

All ages

If you'd prefer to keep your body out of it, there's plenty of plain-old hands-on stuff as well, such as the Cloud Ring Maker and an area where you can use wind to create sand dunes. Children can test their architectural skills—as well as their patience—with the confounding Catenary Arch, which challenges them to build freestanding arches with oversize, soft bricks. The center's first outdoor exhibit, the Solar Fountain, operates on solar energy (a fortuitous installation given the state's recent woes); rotate the solar panels to watch the sun's energy converted into power. Make-and-take activities occur on most days, as do live science presentations. In the near future, look for such exhibits as the Science of Surfing.

Electronic finger painting, story hours, and crafts are among the activities for kids 5 and under at the KidStation; there's also a soft-play area for really little ones. And the whole family's bound to like the 3-D laser theater.

EATS FOR KIDS

Choose between two on-site cuisines at **Taco Bell/Pizza Hut Express** (tel. 714/542–5125). If that's not enough choice, head to the Main Place mall, whose several restaurants include an **Olive Garden** (2800 N. Main St., tel. 714/541–8323).

HEY, KIDS! Are you ready to become an astronaut? Test your readiness for interplanetary travel in the center's Air and Space section. Reaction Time—where you respond to a panel of lights—tests how quick you are. Grip Strength, a self-explanatory test of hand power, is essential for peak space performance. The Manipulator Arm puts you in command—via joystick—of a laser-clad arm, similar to those on space stations. Precision is an astronaut's hallmark. How well can you control its motion?

DISNEY'S CALIFORNIA ADVENTURE

There's nothing like the launch of a new Disney park to make theme park enthusiasts salivate. After roughly half a century, Disneyland, the one and only park that Walt himself built, has finally got a sibling next door.

On 55 acres (the same size as Disneyland when it opened), the new park is, fittingly, an ode to all things California. In three lands, designers have adeptly re-created some of the Golden State's famous sights, from Monterey to Hollywood to the national parks. Rides—and there are some good ones here—are interspersed with less-traditional theme park fare, such as a "tour" of wine country, a walk through a sourdough bakery, and lots and lots of surprisingly good food.

The park has received some criticism for charging the same price as Disneyland for decidedly fewer perks—22 attractions compared to 60 next door—and many of them more appropriate for grown-ups than children. So is this a good choice with kids?

EATS FOR KIDS **Award Weiners,** in the Hollywood Pictures Backlot, has the park's best dogs and fries. At the **ABC Soap Opera Bistro,** also in the Hollywood Pictures Backlot, you can dine in any of six soap scenes. For more options, head outside the park to Downtown Disney.

HEY, KIDS! Don't miss your chance to become an official Junior Explorer. Special maps detail 15 rides perfect for the pint-sized set. After you experience each attraction, pick up a sticker to affix to the map. Collect all 15 stickers, and get a Junior Explorer button plus a card good for discounts in several shops and restaurants. And now for something completely different: The program is free. Look for the Junior Explorer map on the way into the park.

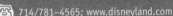

1313 Harbor Blvd., off I-5, Anaheim

$43 ages 12 and up, $33 children 3-11

714/781-4565; www.disneyland.com

M-F 10-6, Sa 9 AM-12 AM, Su 9-9; extended hrs summer and holidays

All ages

The park definitely has some dandy attractions. Hands-down favorites include the magnificent Soarin' Over California, a virtual glider ride that qualifies as a technological wonder. The Grizzly River Run raft ride is a sure pleaser, if you don't mind getting wet. While not a ride, Disney Animation, a journey through the Disney drawing room, delights visitors of all ages. The Paradise Pier section—a remarkably adept re-creation of those turn-of-the-last-century boardwalk amusement areas—is a marvel just to look at, but it's also got a beaut of a roller coaster (California Screamin'), a shoot-you-into-the-heavens gizmo (Maliboomers), and a few kiddie rides. Beware, however: the area also has those maddening win-a-toy carnival games (hint: the fishing game is a guaranteed win, and the prizes aren't bad).

Overall, a visit here makes for a fun day, as long as you're prepared for a nonstandard theme park experience. One of the best parts, in fact, is a slower pace devoid of the characteristic ride-to-ride frenzy. If that sounds appetizing, give into the cost and give it a whirl. Otherwise stick to Disneyland until the kids are older.

KEEP IN MIND Of the two 3-D experiences, Muppet*Vision and It's Tough to Be a Bug!, the former is more appropriate for young children, as the bug show, though funny, can frighten little ones. If you live locally, consider an annual pass, but be warned that there are numerous blackout dates. The park is doable in a day, but don't try to squeeze in Disneyland as well. To stay drier on Grizzly, try to get a seat away from the entry openings. Do not wait more than a few minutes to experience the dreadful Superstar Limo ride.

DISNEYLAND

One of the best things about having a kid is being able to act like one yourself. So though you don't actually need a child to go to Disneyland—solo adults account for a substantial percentage of "guests"—holding a little one's hand legitimizes your own squeals and screeches as you steer around in a flying elephant or speed along in a make-believe rocket ship.

Of course, the really good news is that your children are likely to have an equally splendid time. Commercialism aside, Disneyland is a hoot. If you've got preschoolers, expect to spend much of the day in Fantasyland, where your kids may want to twirl endlessly on the teacups (hot tip: twirl before lunch). Other must-see Fantasyland fare includes Dumbo the Flying Elephant (notorious for long lines but a must for novice visitors), Snow White's Scary Adventures (too scary for some kids), and Storybook Land Canal Boats (magnificent miniatures you won't find at other Disney parks). The talking mailboxes and other interactive gizmos at Mickey's Toontown turn the village into a living cartoon; you may find it hard

KEEP IN MIND Visit in fall or winter, when attendance is lower and the heat is bearable; remember you'll be in direct sun on many lines. If you live locally, consider an annual pass, but be warned that there are numerous blackout dates. You shouldn't budget under a day here. There's *plenty* to do, and it'll take a while to get your money's worth. However, if you visit in summer, get here early and escape at midday, when crowds and heat are at peak levels. Return later to go on rides after little ones have left and for nighttime entertainment and fireworks.

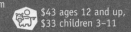 1313 Harbor Blvd., off I-5, Anaheim

 714/781-4565;
www.disneyland.com

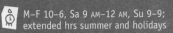 $43 ages 12 and up,
$33 children 3–11

M–F 10–6, Sa 9 AM–12 AM, Su 9–9;
extended hrs summer and holidays

 All ages

to tear little ones away to enjoy the Disneyland Railroad, a vintage steam train that chugs through, among other places, a prehistoric dino land.

The park's "mountain" rides (Splash Mountain, Big Thunder Mountain Railroad, Space Mountain, and Matterhorn Bobsleds—roller coasters all), the Indiana Jones Adventure, and Rocket Rods (billed as Disneyland's longest and fastest ride) are for older kids, if only because of height requirements. As for the other adventures, use your discretion. Star Tours (a flight simulator) and even the Jungle Cruise are going to thrill some little ones, terrify others. One show to be wary of is "Honey, I Shrunk the Audience." The 3-D attraction is a blast for older kids, but younger ones are often reduced to tears. The end-of-day don't-miss for the entire family is the nighttime Fantasmic! show on the Rivers of America. Arrive at least an hour early or be prepared to grab glimpses between the shoulders of the people in front of you.

EATS FOR KIDS
The park has vendor carts and cafeteria-style restaurants, or make a reservation upon arrival at the **Blue Bayou Restaurant.** The **PCH Grill** (Paradise Pier Hotel, 1717 West St., tel. 714/999–0990) offers breakfast with Disney characters, delicious Asian-inspired meals, and entertaining make-your-own pizza.

HEY, KIDS! It looks so innocent from the outside, but don't be fooled by Tomorrowland's Cosmic Wave water maze. You *will* get wet—soaked, actually, right down to your sloshing sneaks. Fountains spurt in changing patterns, surprising you repeatedly, so don't expect a route that looks dry to stay that way very long. Once in the center, see if you can figure out the physics behind the enormous ball on the water pedestal. It moves around easily but, inexplicably, never falls off.

FILLMORE AND WESTERN RAILWAY COMPANY

There's something perfectly peaceful about a train ride through the country. The air is fresh, the scenery is pretty, and, perhaps most important for southern Californians, somebody else is doing the driving. All of that makes a ride on the Fillmore and Western Railway a particularly lovely way to spend a weekend afternoon with the family. Though the views outside the window are not entirely scenic—you'll have to look past low-slung warehouses and homes to fully appreciate the vistas—the mode of transport itself is worth the price of passage.

Trains roll out of the tiny town of Fillmore, a quiet place about an hour north of Los Angeles that looks like time stopped several decades ago. The 2½-hour trip chugs along in vintage 1930s and 1940s cars on a historic stretch of restored, 100-year-old track.

Throughout the journey, passengers can stroll or settle down in several types of rail cars. On warm days, open cars with park benches make for a pleasant way to travel,

GETTING THERE

In general, the recorded and online directions are quite thorough. However, if you're coming from Thousand Oaks, be warned that Moorpark Avenue (Route 23 North) changes to Walnut Canyon Road before winding through the mountains. So don't assume you've made a wrong turn.

KEEP IN MIND

There's ample free parking just outside the railroad's office (the caboose). Reservations are essential, as trains often fill up. You'll also need a reservation to dine on board; dining times are assigned on a first-come, first-served basis at time of boarding, so arrive early if your kids need to eat at a certain hour. You might also want to ask about special Halloween and Christmas trains.

 Central Park Station
(off Rte. 126), Fillmore

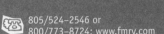 805/524-2546 or
800/773-8724; www.fmry.com

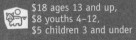 $18 ages 13 and up,
$8 youths 4–12,
$5 children 3 and under

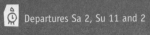 Departures Sa 2, Su 11 and 2

 All ages

particularly since the train never picks up enough speed to whip the wind in your face. Enclosed café cars have tables, and traditional lounge cars look like more modern commuter rails, with oversize, comfy leather seats.

Affable conductors chat up passengers and answer questions about the historic trains. Denim-clad musicians stroll up and down the aisles, strumming and fiddling their way through such travelin' classics as the "Wabash Cannonball" and "Good Morning America." Apart from families, the trip draws a good number of rail enthusiasts, who entertain fellow passengers with their reminiscences of train travel as children.

Eating in the antique dining car is a highlight of the adventure; however, don't wait until you're starving to order, as the service is a bit on the slow side. The train stops in the tiny town of Santa Paula, where you can walk around (tour guides are usually on hand with maps to direct you) before hopping the train for the ride home.

EATS FOR KIDS The burgers, sandwiches, and salads in the old-style diner car are pretty reasonably priced, and the window seats make it a restaurant with a view. Another option is to eat midway through the trip at one of a number of eateries in Santa Paula. One to try is **Famlia Diaz** (245 S. 10th St., tel. 805/525-2813), for homespun Mexican. There are also plenty of restaurants near the station in Fillmore.

FLIGHTLINE

Snoopy isn't the only ace with big dreams of the great blue yonder. If you or your kids have entertained fantasies about soaring the heavens, this is the spot, a place where land-hugging Red Baron hunters can log some pretty lifelike flying hours in the cockpit of the Flightline fleet.

Fittingly located at the Orange County airport, this state-of-the-art flight-simulator center launches aerial daredevil wannabes into the "air," flying in authentically re-created military aircraft. Taxi, take off, and land—preferably in one piece—and you're a success.

The adventure begins with flight suits and helmets—just like standard-issue military uniforms. Next, it's off to the briefing room. Pilots get the lowdown on their aircraft, from basic takeoff and landing to advanced warfare. Pay close attention here: the cockpit is a puzzle of 120 controls, and you wouldn't want to push "eject" when you meant to press "launch missile."

KEEP IN MIND Reservations, particularly for groups, are advised, but drop-ins can sometimes be accommodated. Squadrons (a kind of membership) can cut the cost considerably for frequent visitors, but doing your best in school is required for Squadron participation—a nice touch for parents. Kids too young to pilot can go along as co-pilot, but since you'll have to be confident that your little one can resist banging on all the buttons, the recommended minimum co-pilot age is 8. Older co-pilots can actually help navigate.

17831 Sky Park Circle, Suite B, Irvine

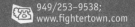 949/253–9538;
www.fightertown.com

 $35; $45 pilot
and co-pilot

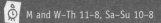 M and W–Th 11–8, Sa–Su 10–8

 10 and up

At last, pilots climb into the bright blue simulators and are sealed into the cockpit beneath a canopy. Then the action begins. Images during your one-hour flight are displayed on monitors inside the jet; screens at the upstairs Officer's Club let onlookers keep watch. Flight controllers offer direction throughout, but pilots take note: it is possible to "crash." Unlike the real thing, however, you're quickly relaunched in a brand-new plane.

"Cadet" (aka novice) programs include taxi, takeoff, and a bombing run. If you're feeling cocky, ask about dogfighting against fellow pilots—perhaps Mom or Dad. But be prepared to apologize after you shoot poor Mom down. On the other hand, it does occasionally happen that Mom blows junior out of the sky.

EATS FOR KIDS
You'll find myriad choices at the nearby Irvine Spectrum (71 Fortune Dr.), including **P.F. Chang's China Bistro** (tel. 949/453–1211). If your kids need more bells and whistles, go to **Dave and Buster's** (tel. 949/727–0555), where arcade games go hand in hand with Americana fare.

HEY, KIDS! So, you think math is just a big bore? Think again. Hitting your missile target requires calculating closure rate, aspect angle, and intercept time—mathematical equations all. Generally speaking, the pilot with the best math skills has the best chance of besting the competition in the dogfight. The moral of the story: Tom Cruise's *Top Gun* alter ego wasn't just an ace pilot—he was a math stud, too.

FORT MACARTHUR MUSEUM

On its perch overlooking the coast, this defunct military fortress is a rare find. With gun batteries (minus the guns), strategy rooms, and tunnels still intact, it is, according to literature, the best-preserved U.S. structure of its kind. Still, from a kid's point of view, this fortified edifice has something equally (if not more!) important than military significance going for it; it's a really cool place to explore.

Built in 1916, Fort MacArthur was the first line of defense against possible invaders off the Pacific Coast. Back then, armed troops stationed here used their vantage point atop the bluff to scope out incoming ships. Pacific Coast threats loomed particularly large early in the century, climaxing at the beginning of World War II, when submarine sightings and red alerts rang out regularly.

There was also a time when an underground fortress was planned, but though many tunnels were drawn up, only a few were built. Children enjoy hunting around for the tunnel

HEY, KIDS!
The weapons are gone, but their legacy lives on. The seacoast guns that once occupied these heavy-duty batteries were capable of firing 14 miles. Despite their mammoth size, these specimens of artillery were handled adeptly by experts who could load, fire, and retract in under 20 seconds.

KEEP IN MIND Just steps away, nonmilitary personnel (seals and sea lions) recuperate from injuries at sea at the Marine Mammal Care Center (3601 S. Gaffey St., tel. 310/548–5677). More nearby history can be found in Wilmington. The 1864 Banning Residence Museum (401 E. Main St., tel. 310/548–7777), home to General Phineas Banning, a founder of Los Angeles, features tours of its mansion, a one-room schoolhouse, and a stagecoach barn, and the Drum Barracks Civil War Museum (1052 N. Banning Blvd., tel. 310/548–7509) is the only Civil War–era army building remaining in southern California.

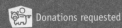
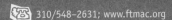
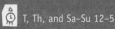

that connects the front of the fortress to the back. But make sure to accompany your youngsters, as it can be creepy in that dark space.

Eventually, the passage of time rendered the outpost obsolete. In the 1950s, the facility became Los Angeles's air defense headquarters, home to more than a dozen short-range missiles. By 1974, Fort MacArthur had had its day as a military installation, but as a museum, it's now come into its own. Music of the 1930s plays throughout, photos and a video presentation document its history, and many rooms appear as they did in the facility's heyday. The austere, cement structure is both a chilling reminder of war and a chilly respite from L.A. heat, even on the hottest summer days. The climb to the top of the two gun batteries—guns have been removed, so you'll have to use your imagination—is indeed steep, but the spectacular view will explain why this site was chosen in the first place. Military reenactments are held the weekend following the Fourth of July. Ask about guided tours.

EATS FOR KIDS The too-cute **Ports O' Call Village** (Sampson Way, tel. 310/547–9977), resembling a New England fishing hamlet, features cobblestone paths and lots of eating and shopping. The **Whale & Ale** (327 W. 7th St., tel. 310/832–0363), a favorite among longshoremen and families alike, has jolly old English food and such American staples as prime rib and grilled cheese. The **Busy Bee Market** (2413 S. Walker St., tel. 310/832–8660) makes some of the best sandwiches in town—including a to-die-for pork sandwich.

GETTY CENTER

If you're looking for a welcoming place to introduce your kids to art, look no further. Though admittedly renowned more for its architecture (an airy, contemporary, Richard Meier–designed structure featuring lots of glass and marble) than its art collection, the grand Getty is an especially good first museum. In fact, designers and programmers took great pains to incorporate younger visitors into the museum's repertoire.

The collection spans centuries of sculpture, manuscripts, photography, paintings, and decorative arts as well as antiquities. To spur dialogue in your family, rent audio guides—personal digital players with kid-friendly prerecorded tours that are recommended for parents, too. Also look for four Art Information (AI) rooms: one in each art pavilion. AI rooms have touch-screen computer stations where you and your children can go on a virtual venture through the museum and learn about many artworks. Knowledgeable docents can embellish what's in the computer and point you toward the collections. Aspiring artists can even try their hand at easels, with still-life subjects set up on tables.

KEEP IN MIND Though admission is free, it costs $5 to park, and you'll need a reservation to do so if you come before 4 on a weekday (weekends do not require reservations). The frenzy surrounding the museum—and the parking—has cooled some, making a visit here feasible even at the last minute. If you don't bring a car—you can get dropped off or take a cab or bus—you don't need a reservation at all.

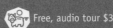 1200 Getty Center Dr., off I-405

 Free, audio tour \$3

310/440-7300

 T–W 10–7, Th–F 10–9, Sa–Su 10–6

All ages

Where the Getty really shines, however, is in its Family Room—ironic considering that progenitor J. Paul Getty was such a misanthrope that he charged his son interest on the money borrowed for his grandson's ransom. Here youngsters can try on costumes resembling the attire worn in famous paintings, check themselves out in the mirror, and then, after removing the clothes, find the corresponding artwork in the galleries. They can explore the art of posing, "try on a new face" via masks, or, as some toddlers do, take a (parent-supervised!) nap. Docents present impromptu demonstrations. Sign out one of the inventive game boxes, offering such educational and fun activities as a museum treasure hunt. The museum also features regular family programs, such as storytelling and workshops, as well as quarterly family festivals with music and dance. If your kids need a break from art appreciation, there's plenty of open space and lovely gardens. If all that fails to make an impression, the tram ride up the mountain is the art-world equivalent of Disneyland's monorail.

HEY, KIDS! The center's marble—one million square feet of it—was brought over from Italy. Virtually every one of the 300,000 pieces on floors and walls has a cool little fossil embedded in it: leaves, flowers, and occasionally a small animal. How many can you find?

EATS FOR KIDS Eating on site is very convenient. Choices include the self-service **cafés,** all of which have indoor and outdoor seating as well as such kid favorites as pizza. The full-service **Restaurant** (tel. 310/440–7300) features some stellar views and its own original artwork, as well as salads, grilled items, and daily specials that appeal to more grown-up palates. Reservations are recommended. If you'd prefer to bring your own, the Getty allows you to dine alfresco in its picnic area.

GRIFFITH OBSERVATORY

Like many other Los Angeles attractions, this planetarium and science center is notable for its celebrity as much as its function. Featured in a scene from the James Dean film *Rebel Without a Cause* and in numerous movie and television productions since, Griffith is one of the most recognized science structures in the country. And no wonder. In addition to its merit as a science center, it has a prime location—high atop a hill in L.A.'s Griffith Park, with incredible views of Los Angeles and the fabled Hollywood sign. The drive up alone makes it worth a visit.

Celestial enthusiasts will be happy to know that Griffith Observatory is more than just a pretty face. Filled with exhibits and activities to learn about meteorites, stars, and the earth, the observatory is a great place to take the family on an exploration of the universe. Along with a Zeiss telescope in the famed dome (available for viewing on clear nights), there are samples of space debris hurled to earth and activities to test your children's (and your) knowledge of the universe, constituting a Constellation Quiz.

EATS FOR KIDS The parking lot **snack bar** serves vending machine–quality food for the truly desperate. Better bets: bring a picnic or down some pasta at either **Louise's Trattoria** (4500 Los Feliz Blvd., tel. 323/667–0777) or **Palermo's** (1858 N. Vermont Ave., tel. 323/663–1178).

HEY, KIDS! Tired of being a kid? Use the Astro Computer to calculate your age in interplanetary years. You'd feel grown up (roughly four times as old) on Mercury, which travels around the sun four times—in other words, four of its years—in the time it takes the earth to go around just once. On the other hand, even your 90-year-old grandma would be young (3, to be exact) on Saturn, which takes 30 of our years to revolve around the sun once.

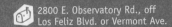 2800 E. Observatory Rd., off
Los Feliz Blvd. or Vermont Ave.

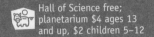 Hall of Science free;
planetarium $4 ages 13
and up, $2 children 5–12

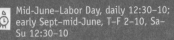 Mid-June–Labor Day, daily 12:30–10;
early Sept–mid-June, T–F 2–10, Sa–
Su 12:30–10

323/664–1191;
www.griffithobs.org

 5 and up

You can even try your hand at creating your own earthquake—a dubious activity in this region. Weight watchers will be delighted to learn what they'd weigh if they lived on the moon (⅙ of their weight here). On the other hand, if you've cheated on the diet this week, you'll want to skip the feature that tells you what you'd weigh on Jupiter.

In addition to its popular Lasarium shows, the planetarium at Griffith offers space exploration daily. Shows here are less of the snooze variety than at some other places, although those expecting an ultraslick extravaganza might be disappointed. Griffith's version is truly educational, but a live scientist cum narrator is comical enough to make it entertaining as well. After all, this is L.A.

KEEP IN MIND Though children of all ages are allowed into the exhibits, those 4 and under are barred from most planetarium shows. However, the afternoon show in summer (usually at 1:30) permits children under 5. Nighttime, particularly in the summer, can bring crowds and parking woes. Arrive at least an hour early if you want to attend either a planetarium or Lasarium show. Avoid the long lines for Zeiss viewing by coming on a weeknight during the winter, as summertime lines can get quite long.

GRIFFITH PARK HORSE RENTAL

46

Miles of roads loaded with shiny vehicles (most of them stuck in traffic jams) have made Los Angeles famous for four-wheeled travel. But the nearby mountains and park trails make it the perfect clip-clopping grounds for four-legged transportation as well.

Short rides head up on the Skyline trail where, if it's a clear day (in L.A., a big *if*), you can see the entire San Fernando Valley. Longer rides can take you as far as Dante's View, where you'll see the Griffith Park Observatory as well as downtown Los Angeles. Other stops include a visit to Amir's Garden, a beautiful expanse of flowers above the valley.

Trail rides can accommodate all skill levels, from novices to pros—as long as you stand over 4 feet tall. Don't be shy about fessing up to being a first timer, though; Old Trigger

KEEP IN MIND In addition to your ride, consider sightseeing on your own two hooves on one of Griffith Park's hiking trails. You can get maps and information from the Ranger Station (tel. 213/665–5188). Be sure to ask about level of difficulty before setting out. There's also a bird sanctuary (open daily 10–5) in the park. For riding opportunities in other areas, try Two Winds Ranch (tel. 805/498–9222), in Newbury Park, or Country Trails (tel. 714/538–5860), at Irvine Regional Park.

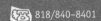 Los Angeles Equestrian Center,
480 Riverside Dr., off I-5, Burbank

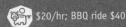 $20/hr; BBQ ride $40

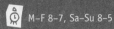 M-F 8-7, Sa-Su 8-5

818/840-8401

 6 and up and at least 4'

can become a mite stubborn if he smells a rookie, so you'll want to ask for a mount that might actually accede to the commands (requests?!) of a beginner. To keep extra comfy, riders should wear closed-toe shoes and long pants, especially for long rides. If you're brand new to the saddle, start with a shorter ride, or you (and your lower half) may live to regret it.

April through October, on alternate Friday nights, the stable hosts BBQ rides that include a 1½-hour guided ride and a barbecue dinner upon return. They start at 6:30 and are available on a first-come, first-served basis; reservations for groups of 10 or more are accepted.

EATS FOR KIDS After a ride in Griffith Park, try **Island's** (117 W. Broadway, Glendale, tel. 818/545-3555) for burgers, sandwiches, and tacos in a colorful tropical atmosphere. A very short trot from the equestrian center, **Viva Fresh** (900 Riverside Dr., tel. 818/845-2425) serves Mexican favorites such as burritos, tacos, and enchiladas.

HOLLYWOOD BOWL

There's more to children's music than Raffi, Barney, and the latest boy band. You just have to know where to look. One place is the Hollywood Bowl, which has been introducing families to music for over three decades. Here you can warm up to classical, jazz and blues at concerts aimed at making music appreciators of us all.

A cultural landmark, the Hollywood Bowl offers an annual six-week Open House, featuring a different performer and style of music each week. Past summers have showcased African drum music, Latin jazz, and southern blues, among others. Recently, the program has taken a historical approach, sampling classical music from different eras. These outdoor events—held not in the main theater but in the shaded patio stage near the museum—have a festival feel. Afterwards, kids can take part in related visual and performing arts workshops that may include crafts. Following a program of southern music, for example, kids created a paper quilt. Occasionally, as was the case after the African drum concert, children can try their hands on instruments similar to those used in the concert.

HEY, KIDS!
After an Open House concert, ask Mom and Dad to bring you into the main amphitheater, especially awesome if the Philharmonic is rehearsing. In the Hollywood Bowl Museum, you can learn about the shell and the people who've performed here—from the Beatles to Christina Aguillera.

KEEP IN MIND Of each day's two Open House performances, the 10 AM Parent and Me Music Making Workshops are for ages 3–5, while the 11:15 show is geared to ages 5–11. In winter the Philharmonic's family concerts, called Symphonies for Youth, move indoors and downtown to the Dorothy Chandler Pavilion (Music Center of Los Angeles County, 135 N. Grand Ave., tel. 323/850–2000), and eventually the Walt Disney Concert Hall (under construction). For 45 minutes before each Saturday-morning concert ($7–$10 each), the lobby overflows with activities. Griffith Park has free concerts through the Symphony in the Glen series (tel. 213/955–6976).

 2301 N. Highland Ave.

 323/850–2000;
www.hollywoodbowl.org

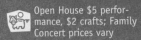 Open House $5 performance, $2 crafts; Family Concert prices vary

 Open House early July–mid-Aug, M–F 10 and 11:15; Family Concerts about 1/mth, times vary

 Open House 3 and up, Family Concert 8 and up

Three orchestras (all under the Los Angeles Philharmonic's umbrella) call the Hollywood Bowl's main amphitheater home in summer: the Los Angeles Philharmonic, which gives adult-oriented concerts on Tuesday and Thursday nights; the Clayton-Hamilton Jazz Orchestra; and the Hollywood Bowl Orchestra, which offers three Family Concerts each season. For a classical freebie, stop by the Hollywood Bowl on a summer Tuesday or Thursday morning; you may get to see the Philharmonic in rehearsal.

Naturally, the choice of music for youth concerts takes young tastes into account, but the format isn't patronizing. In fact, Open House performers are chosen for their educational performance background as well as musicianship, and concerts are entertaining *and* instructive. It's like introducing your children to a new vegetable: You can make them try a bite, but they're more likely to really like it if you disguise it as something else.

EATS FOR KIDS Alfresco diners can either bring a picnic or purchase refreshments and sandwiches at the on-site **stand.** There's a little of everything (sandwiches, salads, etc.) at **Musso & Frank's Grill** (6667 Hollywood Blvd., tel. 323/467–5123), a staple in the area. Grab some good and inexpensive Mexican eats at **Sharkey's** (1716 N. Caguenga Blvd., tel. 323/461–7881). Not too far away are the eateries and people-watching of **Universal Studios CityWalk** (*see* Warner Bros. Studios Tour).

HOLLYWOOD ENTERTAINMENT MUSEUM

The names Sam and Diane may not mean anything to your kids (alas, *Cheers* registers as a golden oldie to children of the 1990s), but sidling up to the famous bar "where everybody knows your name" is still a kick. Original sets from such series as *Cheers* and *Star Trek* are among the treasures of this little museum in the heart of Hollywood—a place where tours, exhibits, artifacts, and hands-on activities give a glimpse into SoCal's "final frontier."

Start at the museum's main gallery, where you'll find an elaborate, six-minute film montage featuring clips of the classics. The film is entertaining not only for its visual beauty (it was pieced together by an Oscar-winning filmmaker), but also for the challenge it poses as you try to name all the films and actors that flash across the giant screens. This is also where you'll find interactive exhibits that explore the craft of movie making—

KEEP IN MIND This relatively undiscovered, uncrowded gem is a fairly quick visit—two hours max. But there are plenty of other things to see outside, including the Hollywood Walk of Fame, Hollywood Guinness World of Records (6764 Hollywood Blvd., tel. 323/463–6433), Hollywood Wax Museum (6767 Hollywood Blvd., tel. 323/462–5991), and the historic Hollywood Roosevelt Hotel (7000 Hollywood Blvd., tel. 323/466–7000), whose photo gallery documents Hollywood's Golden Age. As of 2002, you'll also be in the neighborhood of the new home of the Academy Awards, but don't expect to get in unless you're nominated.

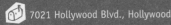 7021 Hollywood Blvd., Hollywood

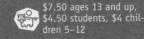 $7.50 ages 13 and up, $4.50 students, $4 children 5–12

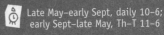 Late May–early Sept, daily 10–6; early Sept–late May, Th–T 11–6

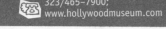 323/465–7900; www.hollywoodmuseum.com

 5 and up

from makeup artistry to character development—and touch-screen computers that detail film history and challenge your knowledge of celluloid lore. In the adjoining Education Center for the Entertainment Arts, tour guides lead editing and Foley (sound effects) demonstrations, allowing a few lucky volunteers to try their hand at putting sound effects to film. It's harder than it looks.

For many, however, the highlight of a visit here is the trip "backstage" to tour the museum's "back lot." You'll see original costumes and props from such film and television productions as *The Coneheads* and *Happy Days*. Your family can amble through a couple of familiar places, including the bridge and transporter room from *Star Trek: The Next Generation,* as well as the entire bar set from *Cheers.* Both sets feature computer touch screens, where you can engage in *Star Trek* trivia or take a look back at some classic *Cheers* scenes.

HEY, KIDS! Sit in Norm and Cliff's bar stools, and hunt for the signatures *Cheers* cast members carved in the bar. Trekkies can see the bridge doors from the original *Star Trek* (unfortunately, they won't open as you approach) and read what those scribbles in the *Enterprise*'s engineering "corridor" really say.

EATS FOR KIDS Hamburger Hamlet (6914 Hollywood Blvd., tel. 323/467–6106), across the street from the museum, serves hamburgers, salads, sandwiches, steaks, and other typical chain-restaurant fare. Ask about discounts sometimes offered with museum passes. About a mile away, dine among L.A.'s famous "dogs," otherwise known as **Pink's Hot Dogs** (709 N. La Brea Ave., tel. 323/931–4223). Hint: they're known for their chili dogs.

THE HUNTINGTON

Its full name is the Huntington Library, Art Collections, and Botanical Gardens—a definite mouthful. But it's an apropros mouthful when you consider all it has to offer. Even if none of the cultural offerings appeal to the littlest ones in the family, the institution's surprisingly liberal and unstuffy philosophy—that its sprawling grounds should be used for "cartwheeling, shrieking and releasing boundless energy"—is bound to be a hit.

Though the atmosphere alone is inviting, the cultural wares here are impressive as well. Founded by businessman Henry E. Huntington, the facility showcases its progenitor's mind-boggling personal collection of art and rare books, including Gainsborough's *Blue Boy,* an original Gutenberg Bible, and a collection of early editions of Shakespeare, to name a few.

More than 100 acres of gardens include a 12-acre desert garden, a lavish rose garden, a tropical jungle garden, and a Japanese garden. The last features a drum bridge

HEY, KIDS!
The koi ponds have been around since the turn of the last century. Generations of turtles have lived here, and many today are descended from those that were here during the Huntingtons' time. Look for baby ducks and friendly koi, too—just please don't touch.

KEEP IN MIND In addition to daily activities, the Huntington offers free nature crafts on the first Saturday of every month 1:30–3:30; no reservations are required. Monthly Children's Garden Workshops, hosted on Saturdays, present different projects each month; past workshops have included flower arranging, bread baking, and papermaking. Reservations and an extra fee, usually around $15 per child, are required. Elementary school kids can take part in weeklong summer programs.

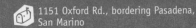 1151 Oxford Rd., bordering Pasadena, San Marino

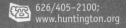 626/405-2100; www.huntington.org

 $8.50 adults, $6 students 12 and up, 1st Th of mth free

 June–Aug, T–Su 10:30–4:30; Sept–May, T–F 12–4:30, Sa–Su 10:30–4:30

 All ages, workshops 7 and up

as well as a traditional Japanese house, the walls of which slide open to afford a peek inside; entry, however, is forbidden.

Organizers here have taken great pains to include children, not just tolerate them. Inside the library and galleries, staff members promote creative ways for children to explore the art and books—perhaps by comparing today's style of dress to what's shown in some paintings or by ambling the mansion, now a gallery, that was once home to Mr. Huntington and his wife. Outside, Plant Discovery Carts help your kids learn about the greenery, while the "Explore!" family guide helps steer your brood through the entire facility. And when your children have had enough of learning about art and literature and nature, you can just relax and watch the abundant small wildlife: ducks and turtles, koi and frogs.

EATS FOR KIDS English tea (frilly dresses optional) is served in the **Rose Garden Tea Room** (tel. 626/683-8131), while the **Rose Garden Café** turns out sandwiches, including PB&Js and grilled cheese. Despite its name, **Burger Continental** (535 S. Lake Ave., Pasadena, tel. 626/792-6634) serves up more than just burgers; Middle Eastern fare and belly dancing are on tap, too. The **Cheesecake Factory** (2 W. Colorado Blvd., Pasadena, tel. 626/584-6000) seems similarly misnamed, since it sells more than just dessert (chicken, sandwiches, salads, etc.).

IRVINE REGIONAL PARK

You want to go for a bike ride; the kids want to get on a horse or pony. On those days when you're looking for a place to make everybody happy, try this sprawling park that combines nature with novelty. According to locals, it's the best kept secret in Orange County. A vast resource of outdoor activities paired with a handful of attractions, it will make your children feel like they've happened on a kind of amusement park in the woods.

At 477 acres, Irvine provides a lot of territory to cover, which you can do on bike or on foot along miles of hiking and biking trails that entwine the park. Playground equipment makes perfect pit stops for swinging and sliding.

However, it's the center of the park where all the action is, including pony rides and a scale-model train ($3) that chugs passengers on a 1-mile loop around a section of the park. Near the train station, at Country Trails Horse Rentals, you can try an even earlier form of transportation on one- to three-hour guided horseback tours around

KEEP IN MIND The open hours of the attractions within the park vary throughout the year, sometimes changing without notice. Many places are open daily in the summer but only on weekends the rest of the year. It's best to call ahead to confirm times (tel. 760/956–8441 pony rides, 714/997–3968 train, 714/633–2022 zoo, 714/289–9616 nature center, 714/538–5860 horseback riding, 714/997–3656 pedal boats). Horseback rides, generally geared to the novice, are typically offered Wednesday through Sunday; reservations are required.

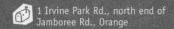 1 Irvine Park Rd., north end of Jamboree Rd., Orange

 714/633–8074; www.ocparks.com/irvinepark

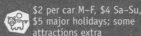 $2 per car M–F, $4 Sa–Su, $5 major holidays; some attractions extra

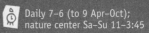 Daily 7–6 (to 9 Apr–Oct); nature center Sa–Su 11–3:45

 All ages, horseback riding 8 and up

the park. A small lake, also in the heart of the park, accommodates anglers as well as pedal boats.

One of the park's real surprises is the small but steadily growing 3-acre Orange County Zoo, home to such native southwestern animals as a black bear, a mountain lion, bobcats, coyotes, armadillos, porcupines, and even a bald eagle and a golden eagle.

More than 100 years old, Irvine Regional Park qualifies as the oldest regional park in the state. You'll learn that fact, along with other information about the park's history and the plants and animals that live here, at the on-site nature center, near the zoo. For example, the park bears the name Irvine—despite its location in neighboring Orange—because the land was originally donated by James Irvine, Sr. Just in case you were curious.

HEY, KIDS! The mewing you hear isn't a cat stuck in a tree; it's a peacock. The birds were brought to the park in the 1970s, and today 50 or so roam freely here, surprising visitors who think they've escaped from a cage. If you're lucky, you may see a male displaying his colorful tail.

EATS FOR KIDS The park was once used by pioneers as a picnic ground, and not a whole lot has changed. You'll find no shortage of places to picnic here. For burgers, hot dogs, and snacks, try one of the **snack bars,** near the lake and in the train station. At the homespun local favorite that is **John's Place** (8400 E. Chapman Ave., tel. 714/997–4292), you'll find Mexican food, sandwiches, and maybe even John.

KIDSEUM

41

On a typical day at this half of a two-part institution (the Bowers Museum of Cultural Art is a couple of doors down), the staff and its visitors were fully immersed in a South Pacific family festival with leis, hula dancing, and all. Needless to say, everyone was having a ball (or should we say a luau?). Such special events occur one Saturday a month at this inventive multicultural learning and play center, where kids can get in on activities (such as those hula-dancing lessons), storytelling, and other endeavors geared to the month's cultural theme.

But don't miss out on the Kidseum's standard fare; the everyday stuff is worth a visit as well. Bright and colorful spaces are strewn with games and play areas. Among the favorites is the well-stocked dress-up area; it literally overflows with garb. The mix-and-match wardrobe of sombreros, Indian saris, Chinese gowns, Colonial dresses, and Dutch wooden shoes, to name just a few, makes for some pretty eccentric ensembles. Kids can keep the clothes

EATS FOR KIDS The full-service **Pan Gata** (2002 N. Main St., tel. 714/550–0906), right inside the Bowers Museum, dishes up California French cuisine. **California Pizza Kitchen** (see the Santa Ana Zoo at Prentice Park), at the Main Place shopping center, serves the obvious fare.

HEY, KIDS! Ever wonder what an Egyptian tomb looks like? The Kidseum's archaeology room is painted to look just like the burial site of Nefertari, wife of Egyptian King Ramses. Whether or not the queen herself was able to appreciate these now-famous murals is up for debate; thankfully, you'll be able to enjoy it while you're alive. In case you're wondering, Anubis, the guardian god of the tomb, is the one with the jackal head.

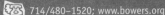

on as they step through the door to the Time Vault (once the bank vault of this old financial building) and take a seat in the stagecoach or saddle (a wooden horse).

Crafts, based on the theme of the month, can be undertaken whenever the museum is open, and the puppet theater area is filled with favorite animal "performers." For less stimulation, there's a quiet book corner for curling up with a good story. Recent additions include an archaeological program (tel. 714/480–1524), in which kids take part in an on-site "dig" and create artifacts to take home; reservations are required.

Though indeed well stocked, the Kidseum is small and intimate enough not to be overwhelming. The staff is particularly amiable, allowing kids to fully explore their imaginations. Noted one smiling worker observing the activity, "As you can see, we're not worried about the kids being neat and tidy."

KEEP IN MIND While you're in the neighborhood, think about stopping by the Bowers Museum (2002 N. Main St., tel. 714/567–3600). Here you can get a look at some amazing ethnic art and artifacts from around the world. Admission to the Bowers includes the fee for the Kidseum, although the reverse is not true. As at the Kidseum, the focus is on cultural history and multiculturalism, but the Bowers is oriented more to adults.

KIDSPACE CHILDREN'S MUSEUM

The creators of this good-size facility seem to have thought very carefully about what amuses kids most, and they were most definitely on the mark.

Pretend play has been taken to the limit. A fire station has full firefighter regalia, a real engine (the back, anyway) complete with hoses, and even a small fire pole to slide down. Kids like to see if they can place the boots just right so they can slide down the pole into them. Little postal workers can sort and cancel mail behind the post-office counter and then take the bag and make deliveries around the room. Expect to be recruited as a customer in the grocery store, modeled after a large California chain. Thanks to a meat counter, lots of "food," and a working cash register with "money," it's about as close to the real thing as you can get without having the milk spoil.

Aspiring news anchors can do weather, sports, and news at the KCBS desk and then watch themselves on the monitor. And a full-size stage comes with dress-up clothes. Longing for

KEEP IN MIND Special events abound: Weekend workshops have featured cooking classes and mariachi dancing, and young children like the Caterpillar Club, Tuesday–Thursday afternoons. Seasonal events include October's Big Haunted House, with in-house trick-or-treating. The Rosebud Parade, just after Thanksgiving, lets kids take part in a mini version of the famed Rose Parade, complete with the Rose Queen and Court. Also look for the Eco-Arts Festival, culminating on Earth Day (April), and the Critter Expo, a display of creepy crawlies such as reptiles and bugs, in early summer.

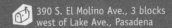
390 S. El Molino Ave., 3 blocks
west of Lake Ave., Pasadena

626/449-9144;
www.kidspacemuseum.org

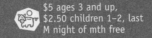
$5 ages 3 and up,
$2.50 children 1–2, last
M night of mth free

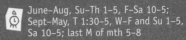
June–Aug, Su–Th 1–5, F–Sa 10–5;
Sept–May, T 1:30–5, W–F and Su 1–5,
Sa 10–5; last M of mth 5–8

2–10

the coast? The indoor "beach," one of the most popular spots in Kidspace, has many of the pleasures of the real thing, including sand, toys, and a cool breeze, courtesy of cranked-up air-conditioning. Additional Kidspace activities include a small crafts area and Robotix, a new exhibit where kids can assemble their own robots and then operate them via remote control. (Unfortunately, Robbie's parts are expensive, so he'll have to stay at the museum when you're done.)

Some exhibits are even alive. Critter Caverns is a kids' dream of a bug and reptile collection. For those who want to get real close (be warned: we're talking snakes and tarantulas, folks), museum staff are often on hand to bring out the creepy crawlers for personal inspection. The Caverns also includes a kid-size climbing area that re-creates some of the animals' natural habitats. So if your children don't want to be with them, they can just be like them.

HEY, KIDS! You've probably seen an ant farm; now find out what it feels like to live in one. The popular InterAntics is a 17-foot climbing sculpture in the form of a human-size ant farm. See if you can make it all the way to the top.

EATS FOR KIDS Old Pasadena, the city's refurbished historic retail district, is full of places to eat, including the **Crocodile Cafe** (88 W. Colorado Blvd., tel. 626/568–9310), which features grills, pastas, and pizzas. Outside of Old Pasadena, in the Lake Avenue retail district, look for **Tony Roma's** (246 S. Lake Ave., tel. 626/405–0612), the well-known chain that serves up tasty ribs and other barbecue favorites.

KNOTT'S BERRY FARM

Out-of-towners may flock to the area's nationally known amusement behemoths, but locals have come to cherish this home-grown favorite. Among southern Californians, Knott's is *the* place for rides: big ones, little ones, and just about everything in between.

Founded in the early 20th century as a berry farm (hence the name), this second-largest California amusement park might as well be called the not-so-little theme park that could. Its six theme areas—Ghost Town, Camp Snoopy, Siesta Village, Indian Trails, Wild Water Wildnerness, and the Boardwalk—comprise more than 165 rides, stage shows, and other attractions. Knott's youngest visitors feel at home in Camp Snoopy, where the Peanuts gang hangs out, and where little rides correspond to little people. There are mini trucks and scaled-down roller coasters, not to mention a bounce house, petting zoo, and miniature steam train. There's also an inventor's workshop, named for a guy called Edison, where you and your kids can tinker with a bunch of gadgets while learning basic science principles.

EATS FOR KIDS
Vendors sell meals, snacks, jams, and even boysenberry punch (Knott's invented the boysenberry). **Mrs. Knott's Chicken Dinner Restaurant** (tel. 714/220–5080) is outside the gate (get a hand stamp to return), and **Chicken to Go,** next door, sells picnic fixings you can eat at Knott's tables and benches.

KEEP IN MIND
Knott's can easily keep your family busy for a full day; if you've got little ones, you might never even make it out of Camp Snoopy. If you think you'll want to return to see more of the park or just to do it all again, ask about season passes for residents. The busiest days are in summer, but you can expect to wait on a few extra lines during special events, such as April's Easter EggMazement, the park's annual Easter Celebration, featuring the Easter Beagle. On those extra hot days, scoot next door to Soak City U.S.A. (8039 Beach Blvd., tel. 714/220–5200), Knott's Berry's new water park.

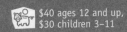
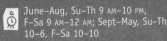

Lest you think the whole park is just for wee folk, Knott's also boasts a renowned collection of frighteningly fun coasters and other rides, including Boomerang (a definite local favorite), Jaguar!, Montezooma's Revenge, and HammerHead. You can just imagine what they're like. Among more recent additions are Supreme Scream, with three seconds of weightlessness while you shoot down 30 stories; GhostRider, a wooden coaster rated one of the world's best by enthusiasts; and Perilous Plunge—incredibly tall, steep, and wet (you'll have to decide whether that's good or not). There are also plenty of equilibrium-annihilating rides with such fitting names as HeadSpin (migraine sufferers will be happy to know that HeadAche has been retired). Beyond those rides made to terrify or nauseate, novel creations include the charming Mystery Lodge, based on Native American stories, and Kingdom of the Dinosaurs, a dark ride back in time. If it's a blistering day, head to BigFoot Rapids, where the white water will more than likely leave you, shall we say, refreshed.

HEY, KIDS! The graveyard over in Ghost Town's Boot Hill boasts headstones from ghost towns throughout the western United States. Legend has it that one of the occupants still has a beating heart. Find it, says the legend—hint, you'll have to step on all the graves to locate the right one—and you'll always have good luck. You can use some of that good fortune when you search for treasure over at the Pan for Gold area of the town.

LA BREA TAR PITS AND THE PAGE MUSEUM

Thousands of years ago, the Los Angeles basin was crowded with mammoths, bison, dire wolves, camels, and enormous 1-ton sloths. The bad news for them is that many wound up stuck in the black gunk that oozes from the La Brea Tar Pits. The good news for us is that their remains have been preserved in fossils that continue to be excavated from the site.

One of the richest sources of Ice Age fossils in the world, La Brea seems to yield an unending supply of immortalized remains. Literally millions of fossils have been recovered since the first documented find in about the mid-1700s, and the discoveries keep on coming. Though you can visit the tar pits year-round, they're idle 10 months a year. During July and August, however, you can watch the annual excavations in Pit 91 from special observation areas set up by the Page Museum, next door. (When strolling near the pits, wear good shoes and walk carefully, as the asphalt tends to ooze up all around.) The finds are pretty amazing, and fossilized bones in the dormant asphalt are sometimes visible to the naked eye.

KEEP IN MIND One note to visitors coming to ogle the site's dinosaur remains: There aren't any. Though dinosaurs are commonly associated with a landscape of bubbling ooze, no dino remains have ever been excavated here, since the pits date back only to the Ice Age (40,000 years ago) as opposed to the dinosaur age (65 million years ago). With membership, you get unlimited admission to the Page, the Natural History Museum, (see #27), and the William S. Hart Museum. Ask about overnights at the tar pits in July.

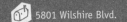 5801 Wilshire Blvd.

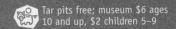 Tar pits free; museum $6 ages 10 and up, $2 children 5–9

 M–F 9:30–5, Sa–Su 10–5

323/857-6311; www.tarpits.org

 6 and up

The bounty of all those finds can be seen at the museum, which is likely to excite most little kids, if only for the chance to see things from so many thousands of years ago. Displays include numerous painstakingly reconstructed fossilized skeletons as well as some millennium-old bones of the tar pits' only human victim ever retrieved. ("Was it an accident or Los Angeles's first murder victim?" asks the exhibit.) On one wall alone there are hundreds of dire wolf skulls, a tribute to just how many animals succumbed to the La Brea site. At the paleontology laboratory, in a nearby enclosure, your children can watch as fossils are cleaned up and preserved, providing a behind-the-scenes look at how all those fossilized clues to the past are pieced together.

HEY, KIDS! In Spanish, *brea* means "tar," so the translation of La Brea Tar Pits is actually the Tar Tar Pits. Though it's repetitive, it certainly underscores the tar's importance. Find out the strength of this gunk at the Tar Vat, where you can try to manipulate a plunger stuck in goo.

EATS FOR KIDS Marie Callender's (5773 Wilshire Blvd., tel. 323/937-7952), a stylish, upgraded link in the chain, contains a bit of vintage decor to accommodate the mid-Wilshire crowd while still offering a large, dependable menu. The **Farmer's Market** (633 W. 3rd St., tel. 323/933-9211) has a characteristically colorful atmosphere and numerous opportunities for alfresco dining. Among the vendors and restaurants here, you'll find everything from seafood to Mexican to deli.

LEGOLAND

I f your single-digit-aged child feels shortchanged by some of the big-name theme parks that seem to cater to older, more adventurous tastes, this full-size theme park made for pint-size dispositions is bound to make a big splash. That's the draw of Legoland. It's 128 acres of things to see and do, all designed expressly for the non-teen set.

About 1¼ hours south of Los Angeles, the park is worth the drive. Apart from its age designation, what sets it apart is its hands-on philosophy. Less a ride mecca than an interactive wonderland, Legoland allows kids to be daring, putting them behind the wheels of boats and mini electric cars they can really drive. The park's driving school, in fact, is the absolute highlight; since the cars aren't on tracks, you catch a glimpse of the future, watching as your children steer, accelerate, and brake (preferably not at the same time), obey traffic rules, and attend to road signs. There's a separate driving school for little drivers ages 3–5. Everyone drives solo (big kids—aka parents—are too heavy for the cars), but don't worry: all drivers have to wear seatbelts). Other kid-motored adventures include the

HEY, KIDS!

Those Technic Coaster cars look like they're made of Legos. And they were—sort of. The four-person vehicles were originally fashioned from colorful blocks. Then designers created a mini Lego version and asked the manufacturer to make it life-size. Imagine the possibilities of *your* Lego creations.

KEEP IN MIND The interactive nature of the park make the rides a hoot—but can mean long lines. Crowds during peak times, in summer and on holidays, can make the experience challenging. The longest lines—Sky Cruiser, the driving schools, and the Royal Joust—are best tried during the lunch hour or shows. Experiencing the whole park should take at least a full day, so plan on closing the park or coming back. Adults can accompany children on all rides except the Royal Joust and the driving schools.

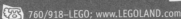
Sky Cruiser, where kids pedal around an elevated track, and the Kid Power Tower, which requires passengers to work together to get to the top. The latest addition, the Technic Coaster, is a two-minute mouse coaster with twists, turns, dips, and a 42-foot drop. (The ride is one of the few with a height requirement: 40".) The newest show, the interactive musical *Life on Mars,* is based on Lego's newest toys.

In case you were wondering if there's actually any Lego here, get ready for the Lego art— 30 million of those famous bricks fashioned into everything from giraffes and dragons to the White House and the Empire State Building. The Enchanted Walk and Safari both feature landmarks and animals made entirely out of Lego. Kids and adults alike have fun sightseeing in Miniland USA, whose many famous U.S. landmarks include the Washington Monument, the Manhattan skyline, and the Golden Gate Bridge. If all of that artwork inspires your youngsters, look for designated areas where they can experiment with Lego and Duplo creations of their own.

EATS FOR KIDS The park's outdoor **Ristorante Brickolini** offers hand-tossed and wood-fired pizza and some unusually tasty pastas made to order, while the **Knight's Table** can fill you up with barbecue favorites. The park's first sit-down restaurant, **Test Track Diner,** serving sandwiches and entrées, overlooks the new roller coaster. Legoland's sweet goodies, baked fresh on property, can be gotten at the **Fun Town Market** or the **Garden Restaurant and Bakery.**

LOS ANGELES COUNTY MUSEUM OF ART

You might think that this exceptional art museum should be your second choice now that the Getty Center has come to town. On the contrary, with more than 150,000 pieces in its permanent collection alone, the Los Angeles County Museum of Art (LACMA, as it's known to locals) has held on to its reputation as the most comprehensive U.S. art collection west of the Mississippi. It's also where you can find some of the more renowned traveling exhibits.

What this means for families is diversity, from Impressionists to Japanese art. Your kids will probably like the Anderson Building's second floor, with its colorful and sometimes playful collection of contemporary art.

Spread across six buildings, LACMA covers a lot of territory. You can amble around the museum on your own or rent an audio tour. Unlike most recorded guides, this one allows you to wander in random order; just punch in the catalog number of the piece you're looking at

KEEP IN MIND Ask about the museum's exceptional extras, such as art, music, and film programs for both adults and children (extra fee required). If you find your kids enamored of the art scene, be sure to find time for another of the area's renowned institutions, the Norton Simon Museum (411 W. Colorado Blvd., Pasadena, tel. 626/449–6840). For art of a completely different sort, try downtown's Museum of Neon Art (501 W. Olympic Blvd., tel. 213/489–0018), the only one of its kind in the world.

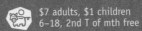
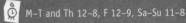

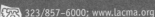
and listen. Only a fraction of the museum's pieces are included on the tour, however, which can be frustrating (new entries are being added). Still, it's a great gimmick for families, particularly since some narration is tagged specially for kids.

The tour is just one way the museum has become increasingly child friendly of late. Among the newest innovations is the Boone Children's Gallery (in the LACMA West building), which has 10,000 square feet of exhibit space geared for kids. Much of what's here is interactive, including video stations, CD-ROM computers, and Discovery Boxes with age-appropriate activities. Hands-on projects are created in the LACMA Lab, and many get kids' whole body into the act; a recent entry allowed youngsters to get into a swing, literally, to create masterpieces. Occasionally, children can contribute to the galleries, such as in the recent So You Want to Be Famous exhibit. Exhibits rotate about every nine months, roughly with the school year.

EATS FOR KIDS The museum's **Plaza Café** serves sandwiches, salads, and hot entrées. Or try the nearby **Marie Callender's** (see La Brea Tar Pits) or Beverly Hills' **Woo Lae Oak** (170 N. La Cienega Blvd., tel. 310/652–4187), where kids can cook food on hibachis at the table.

HEY, KIDS! Many of the great works you know hang on walls or stand on pedestals. But art isn't all paintings and sculpture. In the past, LACMA's collection has included a colorful, larger-than-life billiard set and a great American garage replicated in full detail—right down to an automobile on blocks. Keep your eyes open for things that might surprise you.

LOS ANGELES MARITIME MUSEUM

With concerts, TV tapings, and awards ceremonies galore, Los Angeles is definitely the home of the really big show. But if your child is a boat lover, about the best show in town might just be the one that takes place 365 days a year outside this maritime museum at Los Angeles Harbor.

One of the busiest waterways in the country, Los Angeles Harbor is a stage in constant motion, with everything from tugboats to freighters cruising in and out of her port. You can get a handle on the port's history inside the museum, on the site of a former ferry terminal, where boats to Terminal Island left before the advent of the Vincent Thomas Bridge. Exhibits here highlight the importance of the seaway and outline its roots as a Spanish port in the 18th century.

EATS FOR KIDS Locals rave about the sandwiches at the **Lighthouse Deli** (508 W. 39th St., tel. 310/548–3354). Greasy-spoon comfort food is what you'll find at the **Pacific Diner** (3821 S. Pacific Ave., tel. 310/831–5334).

KEEP IN MIND Before you leave, hop over to the restored S.S. *Lane Victory* (Berth 94, under the Vincent Thomas Bridge, tel. 310/519–9545), a WWII cargo ship featuring tours and memorabilia (separate admission). In addition, several cruises launch each summer. These entertaining family expeditions come complete with the threat of a German spy. Call way ahead for reservations.

Berth 84, foot of 6th St., San Pedro

 Suggested donation $1

 T–Su 10–5

310/548–7618;
www.lamaritimemuseum.org

All Ages

Your kids are more likely to be impressed by the hundreds of ship models, including a detailed scale model of the *Titanic*. Artifacts from the U.S.S. *Los Angeles,* a dismantled navy cruiser, include the ship's bell, a mast, and the ship's flying bridge, which has the added benefit of being a great vantage point for sightseeing. Budding seafarers can test their nimble fingers on the sailor's knot board—there are more than 60 types—or take the (mock) wheel of a 19th-century sailing ship. A working amateur radio station—in touch with operators around the world—shows what global communication used to be like before the advent of instant messaging.

But the real stars are outside on the back deck, where you'll have front-row seats and a close-up view of all the vessels going by. Sit back and watch the changing show.

HEY, KIDS! That big mast outside the museum was once part of a big ship, the U.S.S. *Los Angeles.* One of several navy vessels named in L.A.'s honor, the heavy cruiser weighed more than 13,000 tons and carried among her wares two aircraft and many arms. Commissioned in 1945, she had a distinguished military history. Learn more about the ship from some who manned her at www.USS-LA-CA135.org.

LOS ANGELES ZOO

When the urge comes to visit animals, you could hop in the car and head a couple hours down the 405 to the San Diego Zoo. Or you could stay closer to home at L.A.'s own zoo. More and more folks have been doing the latter, especially since the Los Angeles Zoo has gotten a shining of late. For a pleasant and relatively cost-conscious family afternoon, you'd do well to stay local and visit this animal kingdom in the heart of Griffith Park.

Five distinct "continents" make up the zoo's world: Africa, Australia, Eurasia, North America, and South America. About 1,200 animals are displayed in an up-close fashion that allows you to fully appreciate their height (giraffes) and girth (elephants).

The Chimpanzees of the Mahale Mountains, opened in 1998, marked a rebirth for the zoo. Separated by a pane of glass, two species of primate (human and chimp) get an almost nose-to-nose look at each other. Watching the chest-pounding humans and seemingly bemused chimps, it's hard to tell who's performing for whom. Kids love when a baby chimp does

KEEP IN MIND Though decidedly smaller than the San Diego Zoo, there's still plenty of territory to cover—80 acres—so be sure to put on your walking shoes. If you'd prefer a little help with the long haul, get a daily shuttle pass, which entitles you to hop on and off the shuttle to different areas of the zoo. If it's a scorchingly hot day, go hang out with the koalas in their indoor habitat. The air-conditioned exhibit makes a prime respite for humans as well, and besides, these cute creatures do wonders for any mid-afternoon grumpiness.

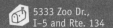 5333 Zoo Dr.,
I-5 and Rte. 134

 $8.25 ages 13 and up, $3.25
children 2–12; shuttle pass
$3.50 ages 13 and up, $1.50
children

 July–Labor Day, daily 10–6;
early Sept–June, daily 10–5

323/644-6400;
www.lazoo.org

 All ages

something they would get in trouble for. The Red Ape Rain Forest, a new, natural home for orangutans, marked part two of the zoo's great-ape forest plan. Other new residents include Gail and Sabor, snow leopards from the Himalayas, and two Sumatran tigers.

Close encounters of the barnyard kind can be had in the new Winnick Family Children's Zoo. Look for goats and alpacas as well as an education center and a nursery for the zoo's newest arrivals. If your tastes range to scaly and slithery, check out the Komodo dragon exhibit. Special exhibitions, such as the World of Birds show, are held during the day, so check your map for a show schedule upon arrival. The zoo is also known for some truly special events, such as its Boo in the Zoo weekend right before Halloween, when kids can go trick-or-treating throughout the grounds. It may not have real ghosts and goblins, but it sure has a *big* black cat (a black jaguar).

HEY, KIDS! When you're up at the glass at the chimpanzee exhibit, put your hand on the glass; sometimes the chimpanzees will match their hand to yours. Which one is bigger?

EATS FOR KIDS There are several places to eat right inside the zoo. **The Grill**, right next to the children's zoo, features burgers, hot dogs, and sandwiches, and indoor seating. **Silverback's Café** has pizza, salads, and Italian sandwiches. Outside the park, **Island's** (*see* Griffith Park Horse Rental) offers a taste of the tropics alongside more traditional fare.

MAGICOPOLIS

In Los Angeles, moviemakers and plastic surgeons get all the credit for creating illusions. But a lady levitating before your very eyes—now that's magic.

Live feats of prestidigitation are on stage weekly at this beach-side Santa Monica theater founded in 1998. Though its designation as "L.A.'s Hot New Magic Club" may have you thinking about acts inappropriate for kids, this hip spot is unquestionably a happy family affair.

The main action is in the Abracadabra Theater, but the fun starts in the lobby, where magicians perform sleight of hand to whet the magical appetite. Inside are the big tricks. Sure, there are always the staples—a vanishing lady, a floating assistant, a sawed-in-half human—but this is anything but old-magic hat. In addition to big and small forms or wizardry, there's music, special effects, and a hefty dose of good humor. There's even a bit of audience participation. The fact that there are no lasers, explosions, or pounding wind machines

EATS FOR KIDS You'll find entertainment (mimes, jugglers) as well as food on the 3rd Street Promenade. A couple of good food choices are **La Salsa** (1401 3rd St. Promenade, tel. 310/587–0755), for Mexican, and **Johnny Rockets** (132 3rd St. Promenade, tel. 310/394–6362).

KEEP IN MIND Magic isn't the only live stage show in the area that's appropriate for kids. For more traditional theater experiences, try the weekly shows at either the nearby Santa Monica Playhouse (1211 4th St., tel. 310/394–9779) or Kelrik Productions (Excalibur Theatre, 12655 Ventura Blvd., Studio City, tel. 818/760–PLAY). Another fun Santa Monica performance venue is Puppetolio (see #19).

doesn't mitigate the amazement factor even a little, particularly since you're watching it live, as opposed to from the living room side of the television screen. Let's face it: Even big televised tricks can be chalked up to trick photography. But in person, even small tricks seem to defy basic laws of nature.

Performances run about 90 minutes and change about every 10 weeks. Owner, magician, and sometime Magicopolis performer Steve Spill lovingly put together the theater from pieces of old buildings. The seats are vintage 1920s, extracted from the old Orpheum Theater in San Diego. Even if you don't appreciate the decor, you're bound to appreciate the stadium-style arrangement, a setup that ensures an unobstructed view for all. Lest you think you may be a long way from the action, the theater's farthest seat is a mere 18 feet from the stage. After the show, learn your own sleight of hand from the Magicopolis shop staff, who sell tricks (many quite inexpensive) and will teach you how to perform them.

HEY, KIDS! There are tons of magic shows but only a limited number of tricks. A real magician, according to Magicopolis owner Steve Spill, only has about a dozen basics up his sleeve, such as making something vanish, reappear, or change position. The real magic is in how he pulls it off.

MARINA PARK'S MOTHER'S BEACH

Lovers of sand and surf have long dubbed southern California's beaches *the* places to be. These, after all, are the beaches of lore, immortalized in song and on screen by the Beach Boys, *Baywatch,* and *Beverly Hills, 90210*. But contrary to popular belief, not all of southern California's coastline is frequented by tanned bodies in bikinis and boxers sporting headphones and multiple body piercings and rollerblading up and down the boardwalk. (For that, *see* Venice Beach.) Some area beaches are actually downright congenial.

If you're looking for the truly tame (in the water and out), you can't beat Marina Park. Located on a quiet stretch past the Alamitos Bay Marina, this is a so-called "Mother's Beach"—characterized by a calm, toddler-friendly current that attracts lots of families. It's the antithesis of the 6-foot-swell-laden beaches that have made California a surfer's heaven; in fact, there are no waves to speak of. The smallish bay beach—one regular

KEEP IN MIND Another Mother's Beach is Marina Beach (Admiralty Way and Via Marina, Marina Del Rey, tel. 310/305–9545). Older kids like the vast sand and activities at Will Rogers State Beach (14800 Pacific Coast Hwy., Pacific Palisades, tel. 310/578–0478 for surf, weather, safety). For surfing, check out Huntington State Beach (21601 Pacific Coast Hwy., at Magnolia Blvd., Huntington Beach, tel. 714/536–1454), home to the International Surfing Museum (411 Olive Ave., Huntington Beach, tel. 714/960–3483), the only place, according to the ad, where it's "OK to call the curator 'Dude.' "

quips that how big it feels depends on how many kids you have with you—is the place for young children to safely splash in the surf or to build sand castles without fear of being swept away by the undertow. Though water gets deeper as you go further out, buoys clearly mark the shallow area, and the drop-off is gradual rather than a sudden plunge. Best of all, watercraft passing outside the designated swimming area are slowed to a mere 5 miles per hour, and speeds are strictly enforced. And, though you must keep watch over your own children, it's nice to know that lifeguards are on duty.

In addition to the de rigeur stretches of sand and water, the park has a playground and a picnic area. If you'd like to use the site for a birthday party (a popular prospect), call the coordinator (tel. 562/570–3215) to make arrangements. Also note that though the beach is free, parking isn't.

HEY, KIDS! How come the waves here are so small? Back in the 1920s and 1930s, a breakwater—an actual barrier—was built several miles off the coast. The breakwater keeps oversized waves from crashing onto the shore, making a perfect playground for undersized sea-goers.

EATS FOR KIDS Refreshments are available from the picnic area's vendor, or you can bring your own. If you'd rather let someone else cook, try the big American menu at **Hof's Hut** (4828 E. 2nd St., tel. 562/439–4775), offering sandwiches, hamburgers, and other traditional family fare. Little ones willing to go beyond PB&Js and chicken nuggets can venture with you to any of numerous Belmont Shores area eateries, including **Super Mex** (4711 E. 2nd St., tel. 562/439–4489), serving fast, good Mexican food.

MISSION SAN JUAN CAPISTRANO

Most people know this southern California mission for its annual ornithological phenomena (the famed swallows make their entrance and exit on March 19 and October 23, respectively) and the resultant 1930s tune "When the Swallows Come Back to Capistrano," which the gift-shop clerk might happily sing for you, if you ask. These days, however, you're more likely to see pigeons here than swallows. Some say that noisy restoration work has sent them away (you'll find lots of nests on surrounding homes—much to some residents' chagrin), but locals hope the swallows will come home to the mission when construction is complete. Still, the 200-year-old Mission San Juan Capistrano—the so-called "jewel" of California's 21 Spanish missions—is a worthy historic adventure nonetheless. Built in 1776, the vast and majestic site feels as grand as an ancient European castle, an enchanting place to soak up some history with your kids while you explore its spacious rooms, exquisite gardens, and ruins.

EATS FOR KIDS The mission's particularly cute town has many eateries. At the **Diedrich Cafe** (31760 Camino Capistrano, tel. 949/488–2150), you can dine in or take out some soup, salad, or a sandwich and picnic in the mission. Nearby, there's a **Ruby's** (31781 Camino Capistrano, tel. 949/496–7829).

KEEP IN MIND Festivals and special events here take full advantage of the lovely surroundings. Saturday evenings June–October, bring a picnic supper and enjoy the outdoor concerts, which start at about 6:30. In February, the Lincoln Festival honors the former president's important role in the mission's history (he signed the document that returned the missions to the Catholic church) with food, activities, and a visit by Mr. Lincoln himself. And of course, the Swallows Festival (March 19 and the weekend before) celebrates the return of the famed birds to the area, if not just the mission. Check the Web site for a complete calendar.

Ortega Hwy. and Camino Capistrano,
off I–5, San Juan Capistrano

 $6 ages 12 and up,
$4 children 3–11

Daily 8:30–5, Living History Days 2nd
Sa of mth 10–2

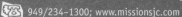 949/234-1300; www.missionsjc.com

 All ages

You're first struck by the ruins of the Great Stone Church, one of the elements that lends the place the feel of another era. History is so well preserved here, in fact, that it's a shock to see the taco stand sign sticking up over the outside wall. Strolling around, it's easy to imagine life here a couple of centuries ago. Some of the more interesting spots include the old Soldier's Barracks, built to house the few military men who were stationed here long ago; the mission cemetery; the Serra Chapel; and the small museum depicting life at the mission. In the ethereal Sacred Garden, 18th-century bells hang in graceful archways.

Although you can visit any time, the best way to get a feel for the place is to come on a Living History Day, held once a month. On those days, volunteers appear in colorful period attire; adopt the character of Spanish soldiers, Juaneño Indians, and other former mission residents; and interact with visitors.

HEY, KIDS! Look for bird-food dispensers spread around the mission. A handful of feed costs 25¢; if you're brave (and fortunate), birds will come and eat directly out of your hands. Over the years, these well-fed birds (feathered friends here, are, shall we say, on the stout side) have become accustomed to their two-legged friends. Birds will land on your shoulder and in your hair. But beware: They're not potty trained.

MOVIELAND WAX MUSEUM

Celebrity may come and go, but a wax figure lasts forever (unless someone gets too close with a match). Offbeat but well done, the enterprise is one of a couple of wax museums in Los Angeles (see the Hollywood Entertainment Museum) that have become a staple of southern California tourism. Included are incarnations of many past and present luminaries, from Michael Jackson (replete in his original "Bad" video ensemble) to John Wayne, Dorothy to President Clinton. Though some may call it hokey (and it is a little), it does make for a fun afternoon. And there is something marvelously intriguing about just how real these wax folks can seem.

All the exhibits have themes, many featuring music and dialogue. Among the most elaborate ensembles are the original *Star Trek* crew standing in the Starship *Enterprise*'s bridge and the depths of the ship in the *Poseidon Adventure*. In a similarly soon-to-be-doomed *Titanic* scene, Leonardo DiCaprio and Kate Winslet are perched aloft the liner's bow. Some of the figures here are amazingly lifelike: Dick Martin, half of the Rowan and Martin comedy team,

KEEP IN MIND A leisurely stroll through the museum will take a couple of hours. If you're feeling energetic, pair Movieland with the Ripley's Believe It or Not! Museum (see #16), across the street. A combined ticket to the two museums will actually net you a discount; you'll have to use half the day you buy it, but the other ticket is good indefinitely. The busiest times at this museum are during school breaks, but even a summer visit can be surprisingly crowd-free and can make for a nice air-conditioned interlude to boot. Ask about educational programs; advance sign-up is required.

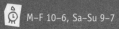

and Bette Davis, to name two. Others are, shall we say, less than true to their originals, but dissing is half the fun. So is some funky trivia.

If all those movie-star smiles aren't scary enough (check out those teeth on Donny and Marie), there's a collection of truly frightening figures in the Movieland Chamber of Horrors, where Jason of *Friday the 13th* fame looks real enough to raise neck hairs. Not everyone will be enamored of the creepy critters, and some kids may be downright terrified. Fortunately, you can skirt the scream theme altogether by following the arrows. Alas, the detour leads you into another house of horrors, a vast bulk candy shop. In fact, shops are interspersed throughout the Movieland experience, including one where future candle makers can get educated in the art of wax figures. Be sure to stop on the way out to see the photo with George Burns you posed for on the way in. There's an extra charge for purchase, though.

HEY, KIDS! You think doing *your* hair is hard? Consider this; wax figures must have their tresses attached strand by strand. The average hair count (not counting Michael Jordan) numbers in the tens of thousands and takes "hair dressers" four–six weeks to complete. Now that's high-maintenance hair.

EATS FOR KIDS PoFolks (7701 Beach Blvd., tel. 714/521–8955), right next door, serves virtually every incarnation of chicken you and your kids can imagine. At **Claim Jumper** (7971 Beach Blvd., tel. 714/523–3227), families can ogle the wild-game heads on the wall while eating hearty portions of pork ribs, hamburgers, fish, and steaks. Also see dining entries in Ripley's Believe It or Not! Museum.

MUSEUM OF FLYING

In the annals of childhood imagination, playing pilot ranks right up there with being a firefighter or a western cowpoke. So it stands to reason that the Museum of Flying is a mighty popular place among families. Fortunately, it takes its role as educator and entertainer to, well, new heights. A diverse collection of things you can get into, steer, and experiment with, the museum is one of those places families like to come back to over and over, if only to master some of its gadgets.

Located alongside the Santa Monica Airport runway, the museum is immediately striking for its display of colorful World War II–era planes (originals and replicas) suspended overhead and parked on the ground. War veterans and kids alike seem captivated by these aluminum and steel legends, most of them still in working order, including such biplanes as the *Yellow Peril* Navy plane and the bright orange 1932 WACO. Of particular pride to the

EATS FOR KIDS Colorful **Acapulco Mexican Restaurant** (3360 Ocean Park Blvd., tel. 310/450–8665) serves Mexican and American food. **Coco's Family Restaurant** (3440 Ocean Park Blvd., tel. 310/450–6257) has diner-style favorites for everyone.

HEY, KIDS! If you're in the mood for action, look for flight-theme arcade games as well as the vintage Armed Service Gunnery Trainer, essentially the equivalent of an old-style video game. A stationary simulator will give you the experience of sitting inside a cockpit, but if you're roughly 5 to 10 years old, you can pilot a moving flight simulator. Using joysticks and pedals, you can operate the flaps and rudder and cause the plane to bank left and right.

museum is the *New Orleans,* one of the first planes to fly around the world. (Its companion plane is displayed at the Smithsonian's National Air and Space Museum.) Active runways just beyond the open hangar door provide for perfect views of takeoffs and landings by small jets, helicopters, and even some of the museum's stock of restored antique aircraft, such as the Japanese Zero Warbird and a P-51 Mustang (both rare originals).

Inside the museum are plenty more interactive exhibits, including simulators, an activity about the science of flying, and a helicopter and replica cockpits that kids can actually sit in. These even have some working parts, which can entertain imaginative children for some time. Upstairs, you can all get a better look at the suspended planes and use headphones to listen in on air-traffic controllers at both the Santa Monica and Los Angeles airports. Getting your kids back down to earth might not be so easy.

KEEP IN MIND Feel free to ask questions of the knowledgeable volunteer docents. Also inquire about the upstairs movie theater, which shows short subjects (roughly 15 minutes)—from documentaries to Blue Angels stunt films to an occasional Charlie Brown picture about the history of flight. As for the moving flight simulator, be warned that the sensation of motion thrills some kids and terrifies others, so prepare your children accordingly. If you're here on a quiet day, the docents are likely to allow a longer "flight."

MUSEUM OF TOLERANCE

The metal detector and bag search at the door is a reminder of the sensitive subjects tackled inside. Though not a typical entertainment stop, this museum is a must-see nonetheless. Educational, fascinating, and occasionally gut-wrenching, the museum explores racism, bigotry, and the Holocaust in a package that's sure to engender conversation.

Though the museum dwells considerably on the Holocaust, it devotes equal time to present-day racism and bigotry. Hands-on activities in the Tolerancenter allow you and your family to explore human-rights violations both abroad (the former Yugoslavia) and at home (the American civil rights movement). More strikingly, though, it encourages kids to consider their own prejudices and stereotypes. The Manipulator, a videotaped man who greets you by voicing extreme prejudices, is disarmingly effective at this.

The elaborate Holocaust section is unforgettable, exploring World War II Germany by immersing you in events leading up to the war. The section is disarming and chilling,

KEEP IN MIND During the school year, avoid mornings, which are often sold out with school groups. In fact, to guarantee admittance, call ahead to purchase tickets. Be prepared for the dramatic film clips, some of which contain stark images—too graphic for children under 12. The Museum of Tolerance features daily speakers, including occasional visits by a former neo-Nazi skinhead, as well as talks by Holocaust survivors Monday through Wednesday at 1, 2, and 3 (call ahead to confirm the schedule).

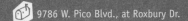 9786 W. Pico Blvd., at Roxbury Dr.

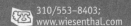 310/553–8403;
www.wiesenthal.com

 $9 ages 11 and up,
$5.50 students and
children 3–10

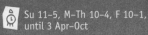 Su 11–5, M–Th 10–4, F 10–1,
until 3 Apr–Oct

 12 and up

particularly the macabre recorded reenactment of the famed Wannsee Conference, during which Nazi officers casually discuss the "Final Solution" and the best method for disposing of their victims. Passport Cards, drawn by visitors at the outset of the exhibit, document the travails of various European children affected by the war; a computer printout at the end reveals the fate of the child you picked.

Overall, the museum's strength is how it humanizes its subjects. Through dramatic film montages, many created by Oscar-winning filmmakers, formerly faceless Bosnian, Jewish, and American civil rights movement victims—and even the perpetrators—become individuals. That hate groups now have a worldwide podium thanks to the Internet is the museum's latest focus. The timely Globalhate.com exhibit alerts budding Web surfers to the thousands of current hate sites and, through photos, gives an eye-opening account of the kind of hate crimes that have been taking place nationwide.

HEY, KIDS! You can't always judge a Web site by its address. Though a Martin Luther King site displayed at the Globalhate.com exhibit may look like a research center, it's really home to a white supremacist group. Lots of these organizations target kids, so beware.

EATS FOR KIDS **Bob Morris's Beverly Hills BBQ** (9740 W. Pico Blvd., tel. 310/553–5513) serves tasty barbecue right next door to the museum. Ribs, chicken, and pulled-pork sandwiches all leave you licking your fingers. **Factor's Famous Deli** (9420 W. Pico Blvd., tel. 310/278– 9175) dishes up super-size delicatessen sandwiches stuffed with salami, pastrami, and more.

NATURAL HISTORY MUSEUM

People are often surprised to learn that the city best known for movie stars and glamour also has one of the largest natural history museums in the country. Number three behind the Smithsonian's National Museum of Natural History, in Washington, and New York's American Museum of Natural History, Los Angeles's Natural History Museum captivates kids with examples of nature from prehistoric to modern, including dinosaur bones, shark skeletons, and live insects.

You're greeted outside by bronze casts of a couple of dueling dinos. Inside are the real things—well, real bones anyway. Huge reconstructed beasts—a T-Rex and a triceratops posed in combat—prompt jaw-dropped stares, and occasionally some frightened whimpers, from kids astonished by the fabled creatures' actual size.

There are more remains all along the Dinosaur Hall on the way to the Discovery Center, where your kids can touch a dinosaur skeleton, dig for fossils in a sand pit, and

HEY, KIDS!

Ever wonder what dung beetles eat? Let's just say their diet makes them the consummate bottom feeders. How about tarantulas? The hairy guys subsist on such delicacies as grasshoppers; the big ones (we're talking up to a foot!) have been known to down the occasional mouse.

KEEP IN MIND Annual membership at the Natural History Museum is a particular bargain, because it also covers unlimited admission to the Page Museum (see the La Brea Tar Pits) and the William S. Hart Museum (24151 San Fernando Rd., Newhall, tel. 661/254–4584), a mansion and ranch that once belonged to the former Western film star. In addition, you'll get mailings detailing an unbelievable collection of family overnights and adventures. Check out the museum each May, when it holds the annual Insect Fair, the largest event of its kind.

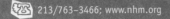

make crayon rubbings from a fossil rock. Little kids often flock to a collection of taxidermic animals they can actually touch. The lion—dog-eared from many years of being loved—seems to be a particular toddler favorite. Older kids can engage in tasks set forward in activity boxes. Thirty-two live animals reside here, too, including an iguana and a 12-foot (caged!) python.

Once you've torn your children away from the Discovery Center (a major feat for most kids), you can head to another favorite: the Insect Zoo, home to such crawly critters as tarantulas, cockroaches, stick bugs, millipedes, and centipedes. Though moms and dads may cringe, the "ick" factor seems to be lost on kids, who have been known to spend many hours getting to know their eight-, 10- and 100-legged friends. Other hot spots in the museum include the Gem Vault, containing rubies, diamonds, etc. (talk about your L.A. rock stars!), as well as the marine and bird halls.

EATS FOR KIDS The museum itself has the **Curator's Cafe,** a cafeteria-style restaurant with salads, hot dogs, and macaroni and cheese as well as special items of the day. On Figueroa, look for **Margarita Jones** (3760 S. Figueroa St., tel. 213/747–4400), a Mexican restaurant that features food for adult and kids' tastes. Ask about the specialty of the house, the *carne asada* (broiled beef).

OCEAN INSTITUTE

One family calls Dana Point Harbor the home of the pirate ship. The two-masted vessel in question is actually an exact replica of the brig *Pilgrim*, the 19th-century ship famous for carrying Richard Henry Dana, Jr., (author of *Two Years before the Mast*) on his perilous journey from Boston to California. (The word "brig" refers not to the *Pilgrim*'s jail but to its rigging—the configuration of sails—during the mid-1800s.) The fantasy-inspiring tall ship, owned by the Ocean Institute, opens its gangway to tourists most Sundays, allowing kids to explore the ship's many nooks and crannies as well as to visit with its crew of sailors, decked out in 1830s period attire.

But there's more to the institute than the period sea vessel. Like Dana himself, families can become explorers, tagging along with the institute's staff of marine biologists as they study the ocean on a state-of-the-art research vessel, the R/V *Sea Explorer*. While on these 1½- and 2½-hour educational cruises (including some on weekend evenings), you'll see not only sea lions and other playful creatures, but also lesser-known inhabitants of the

EATS FOR KIDS **John's Fish Market** (34665 Street of the Golden Lantern, tel. 949/496–2807) is known for fresh, inexpensive seafood enjoyed indoors or out. Apart from the food (burgers, sandwiches, salads), the calling card of **Proud Mary's** (34689 Street of the Golden Lantern, tel. 949/493–5853) is stellar coastal views. You can dine inside or out here, too. The **Brig** (34461 Street of the Golden Lantern, tel. 949/496–9046) serves burgers, seafood, sandwiches, and, on Mondays, all-you-can-eat ribs.

24200 Dana Point Harbor Dr.,
Dana Point

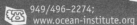 949/496-2274;
www.ocean-institute.org

Pilgrim free; marine
cruises $22 ages 13 and
up, $15 children 4-12

 Lab/whale room Sa–Su 10–4:30; *Pilgrim* most
Su 10–2:30; marine cruise F–Su, hrs vary

4 and up

waters. Some of the most eye-popping finds, in fact, are uncovered when the trawl net comes up with creatures that live on the bottom. Biologists also throw out a plankton net—you'll get to look at what's caught under a microscope—as well as another that trawls for fish.

Half the fun of these cruises is that you never know what you might see. Though the boat runs year-round, you'll get a fringe benefit if you travel January–April. That's when the Pacific gray whales make their annual migration. An up-close look at these majestic creatures is truly awe-inspiring. Whatever you see, though, you can count on getting completely caught up in the experience. The amiable marine biologists seem to truly revel in sharing their work with young explorers and pepper the entire adventure with their infectious enthusiasm. Once back at port, stop by the institute's touch tanks (in the Lab and Whale Room), where you can handle resident sea creatures.

HEY, KIDS! How big is a giant squid? No one knows, since they live in the ocean depths. Estimates are based on squid appendages found at the surface. The 19-foot tentacle here (displayed Sundays only) came from a nearly 40-foot gargantuan. Makes you glad they live way down deep.

KEEP IN MIND It's best to reserve spots on a cruise two to three weeks in advance, but last-minute reservations, even in season, are sometimes available. Be sure to bring your bikes. A 3-mile trail goes all the way from the harbor to Capo Beach; halfway there, at Doheny State Beach, you can rent a surrey, a pedal-powered cart. A sailing ship, a research boat, a bike, and a surrey sure make for a day of varied and interesting transportation.

OLVERA STREET

Most people think of the heart of Los Angeles as Hollywood, but the City of Angels has its roots here, on and around Olvera Street, a place that's been brimming with life since long before the first movie director yelled, "Action."

Settled in 1781 by 11 Mexican families, Olvera Street—now home to the El Pueblo de Los Angeles Historical Monument—heralds its heritage in particularly colorful style. The retail area (created as a tourist attraction in 1930) mimics the charm of a traditional Mexican marketplace, with numerous shops and vendor stands selling everything from clothing and hats to piñatas and hand-crafted pottery. Visit on weekends and you may also happen upon mariachis and folkloric dance troupes. Of course, half the fun of coming here is eating, and there's plenty of that, too. In addition to a few sit-down restaurants, there are numerous homespun proprietors pedaling authentic Mexican fare—the real heartburn-inducing versions—including burritos, tacos, and taquitos.

KEEP IN MIND Call ahead, as establishments here often adjust hours. You can also explore other L.A. ethnic centers, including nearby Chinatown (about a minute's walk from Olvera Street) and Little Tokyo, which features the Japanese American National Museum (369 E. 1st St., tel. 213/ 625–0414).

EATS FOR KIDS There are lots of restaurants to choose from all along Olvera Street. **La Golondrina** (17 W. Olvera St., tel. 213/628–4349), one of the area's largest eateries, features specialty Mexican entrées, such as *mole poblano* (chicken with chilis and nuts and chocolate sauce) and traditional Mexican fajitas. People go to **El Paseo** (11 E. Olvera St., tel. 213/626– 1361) for the fresh, handmade tortillas and gua-camole, as well as enchiladas, tostadas, and other entrées. Both offer indoor and outdoor seating.

Olvera St. and environs, near Union Station

 Free

 Avila Adobe daily 10–3; marketplace daily 10–7; tour W–Sa 10, 11, 12

213/628–1274 area visitor's center; www.olvera-street.com

All ages, tour 10 and up

On both sides of the marketplace are historic buildings. You can get to know them either on your own or on a free 60-minute guided walking tour. Either way, you'll want to hit a few significant stops, most notably the Avila Adobe (10 E. Olvera St.). Built in 1818, this oldest home in Los Angeles is frozen in time, with everything as it was nearly 200 years ago. The Sepulveda House Museum (622 N. Main St.) is an old Eastlake Victorian boardinghouse containing exhibits and showing an 18-minute video on the history of Los Angeles, and the old Plaza Firehouse Museum (134 Paseo de la Plaza) is the city's oldest firehouse. The Old Plaza (1825), formerly the town square, features statues and plaques paying homage to the area's founders and hosts frequent music and dance concerts, with performances ranging from folklore to Latin rock. Our Lady Queen of Angels (535 N. Main St.), also known as the Old Plaza Church, dates back to 1818 and is the oldest in L.A. Still an active Catholic parish, the church is open daily for on-your-own tours.

HEY, KIDS! Throughout the year, the community celebrates traditional and colorful Mexican festivals and holidays. In April, let Fido be the center of attention at the Blessing of the Animals. On this day, people bring in their pets—anything from the family dog to a pet pig to your favorite snake— to be blessed by the Catholic Church. The day-long event, an ancient Spanish tradition, is held on the Old Plaza and starts with a parade and the traditional blessing rite.

PACIFIC PARK

I f you're going to go to an amusement park, why not make it a park with scenery? That's what you'll get at Pacific Park, a charming seaside recreation area sitting right at the edge of the Pacific Ocean on the walkway of the Santa Monica Pier. It has that throwback feel of old-time amusement areas, with rides, restaurants, and junk food, not to mention classic carnival-style games where you can throw basketballs or spray squirt guns to win gloriously homely stuffed animals.

Pacific Park is a descendant of the old Looff Pleasure Pier, which closed in the 1940s. (The Looff Carousel at the entrance to the pier is actually a vestige of the original.) In 1996, an infusion of cash brought the place back to its original splendor, and more recently, the boardwalk atmosphere has been plumped up by the continuing flow of new attractions designed to appeal to the more adventurous, as well as the pint-size, amusement park enthusiast.

KEEP IN MIND Pacific tends to change its hours seasonally. In addition, during off-season (roughly the day after Labor Day to the day before Memorial Day), Pacific Park offers limited operations, meaning only a few rides and games are open (the Ferris wheel, however, always runs). Call ahead for specific times and attractions. Finally, while the pier is definitely a nice place to spend an afternoon, expect those ride prices to add up. If you forgot the skates and cycles, rent them at Sea Mist Rentals (1619 Ocean Front Walk, tel. 310/395–7076).

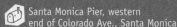 Santa Monica Pier, western end of Colorado Ave., Santa Monica

 310/260–8744, www.pacpark.com; Ocean Discovery Center 310/393–6149, www.odc.ucla.edu

 Free, attractions $1.25–$4 each, Ocean Discovery Center $3

 Mem Day–Labor Day, Su–Th 11–11, F–Sa 11 AM–12:30 AM; early Sept–late May, M–Th 12–7, F 12–12, Sa 11 AM–12 AM, Su 11–9

 3 and up

Stalwarts among Pacific's 12 rides include the 130-foot-tall Ferris Wheel, from which you can all but see forever (those afraid of heights need not apply). A 55-foot-high roller coaster offers additional views, but at only 35 mph, don't expect super thrills. Bumper cars include a version for adults and a mini one, creatively named PCH Driving School, expressly for kids. The new LaMonica Swing thrill ride gives a new spin (literally) to the playground staple. This one's for big kids; little ones will have to settle for Clown Around, a mini version. Also recently debuted, Pier Patrol has "super trucks" (à la *Baywatch*) scaled down for pint-size "drivers." Be sure to look out for some of the park's live entertainment, and don't forget to bring the bikes and blades; just off the pier lies some of the best paved beach-side trails for wheeling and rolling along.

EATS FOR KIDS
The pier has everything from hot dogs to seafood. Within walking distance, **Johnny Rockets** (1322A 3rd St., tel. 310/394–6362) has burgers that are hits with kids, and the **Crocodile Café** (101 Santa Monica Blvd., tel. 310/394–4783) serves up color-in menus alongside American favorites.

HEY, KIDS! Did you know that there's no such thing as a jellyfish? The jiggly guys are actually not fish at all, but rather sea animals in a class all by themselves. Marine biologists are baffled as to where the misnomer came from ("It just stuck," says one) but have recently mounted efforts to correct it. Find out about "sea jellies" as well as other creatures of the Santa Monica Bay at the Ocean Discovery Center, underneath the Santa Monica Pier. Don't miss the chance to watch the sharks eat their squid meals; ask about feeding times on the way in.

PALACE PARK

Video games never looked like this when we parents were kids. (Remember Pong?) A virtual playground of the highest order, Palace Park—easily identifiable from I-405 as the building that looks like a castle—is the place for your kids to go to "buzz," "beep," and "whirr" to their heart's delight.

At 11 acres, Palace Park is one of the largest family entertainment center/arcades in the area. The arcade section looks like a computer-age casino, with electronic boxes lined up row by row and kids and adults careening, steering, and shooting around virtual ski mountains, speedways, and jungles. The cacophony of electronic sounds can be overwhelming, but once in front of the screen, it's hard to tear yourself or your children away. From jet skiing to playing football to dinosaur hunting, the games involve you completely. Races can be run solo or hooked up to challenge others. Each game dispenses tickets (commensurate with your score) that can be traded in for prizes at the on-site redemption center.

KEEP IN MIND Ask about passes that cover all the attractions (the kids' pass applies to kids' rides only) plus two-for-one tokens. Currently, games use one to four tokens, but that could increase as games become more sophisticated. In any case, you can go through a lot fast. (Using 12 tokens and getting 24 tickets in 15 minutes is typical.) Lest you think you'll get something wonderful for all that money, think again. Though some prizes cost five tickets, the big ones will probably cost more than you have. For example, an enormous stuffed bear requires a mere 11,000 tickets. Palace Entertainment, Palace Park's owner, operates numerous other parks in the area; call for locations.

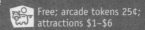 3405 Michelson Dr., off I-405, Irvine

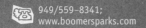 949/559-8341;
www.boomersparks.com

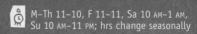 Free; arcade tokens 25¢;
attractions $1–$6

 M–Th 11–10, F 11–11, Sa 10 AM–1 AM,
Su 10 AM–11 PM; hrs change seasonally

3 and up

Next door, laser tag enthusiasts can pursue their sport in particularly elaborate style. The 3,000-square-foot arena—lauded by many fans as the best of its kind—is replete with fog machines, not to mention plenty of places to duck and hide from the "enemy." Also indoors is a flight-simulator ride; outside, look for go-carts, bumper boats, batting cages, and miniature golf. Other outdoor attractions include a 32-foot-high rock-climbing wall and a skateboard park with a street course and half pipe. (If all that isn't enough, you can traipse next door and line 'em up for some old-fashioned entertainment—bowling—at Irvine Lanes.)

Though particularly popular among teenagers, Palace Park has taken care to ensure that the whole family can get involved. Most rides allow riders as small as 42" (there's even a miniature go-cart just for them), and there are plenty of scaled-down arcade games that little ones can play for prizes.

EATS FOR KIDS There's a **McDonald's Express** (tel. 949/759–8517) right inside, serving the fast-food giant's standard fare. Just up the street in the Park Place Plaza complex, you can choose from scads of popular chain restaurants, including **Left at Albuquerque** (3309 Michelson Dr., tel. 949/757–7600). Its southwestern menu includes special children's selections.

PARAMOUNT RANCH

This dusty Old West "ghost" town in the Santa Monica Mountains looks like every gunfightin', shoot-'em-up, corral town you've ever seen on TV or in the movies. And there's good reason for that. A fixture here since Paramount built the place in 1927, the town has been featured in numerous big- and small-screen hits, including *The Flintstones, Cousin Skeeter,* and *Dr. Quinn, Medicine Woman.* That the *X-Files* recently shot here gives the term "ghost town" a new meaning. Cinematic purists will be happy to know that such old-time classics as *The Adventures of Marco Polo* and *The Cisco Kid* were filmed here as well.

Your children will probably be more fascinated by the way the town looks, however, than by what's been shot—or should we say filmed?—here. Resembling a true relic abandoned after the days of stagecoaches and covered wagons, the town is dressed up or down depending on what, if anything, is being filmed. If you're lucky, you might actually catch a production in progress.

KEEP IN MIND To learn about the movie and television history made here, come the first or third Saturday of the month at 9:30, when rangers lead free one-hour "Set to Screen" tours. You can also soak up the atmosphere during a festival, such as the Topanga Banjo Fiddle Contest (May) or the Calabasas Pumpkin Fest (October). Or pack the fishing pole and try your luck at tranquil Troutdale (2468 Troutdale Dr., tel. 818/889–9993). The ranch can get extremely hot in late summer; it's a good idea to bring water and a snack, though there are on-site water fountains, too.

Cornell Rd., Agoura; www.nps.gov/samo

 Free

 Daily 8–sunset

 805/370-2301

All ages, hike 6 and up

Though it's all movie illusion, the Paramount Ranch nevertheless feels authentic, emitting that haunting, ethereal feel of a real-life ghost town. All the cliché establishments are here: feed and grain store, saloon, hotel, train depot, and livery (the names may change—the sign of a recent shoot). All that's missing are horses, and you might see those here, too. A picnic on the train platform really makes you feel as if you're in another era, and all those second-floor railings look like prime places for cowboys to come busting through at the climax of a good gunfight. Though the shops are all closed for business, the exteriors make for great photo ops and imaginative play.

Apart from the in-town scenery, the ranch has plenty of scenic hiking trails, including the ¾-mile Coyote Canyon and Medea Creek trails and the more difficult ½-mile Overlook trail. All are open to hikers, some to horseback riders; call ahead to confirm.

GETTING THERE Getting to the ranch requires careful navigation. Take the Ventura Freeway (U.S. 101) to the Kanan Road exit. Travel south on Kanan for ¾ mile, turn left on Cornell Way, and veer to the right. The entrance is 2½ miles down Cornell Road on the right.

EATS FOR KIDS Though the town is indeed abandoned, there are plenty of picnic benches around (as well as rest rooms). You can count on being plenty hungry after a hike in them thar hills. Down some burgers at **Johnny Rockets** (5015 Cornell Rd., Agoura Hills, tel. 818/879–9933), or fill up on pizza at **Pizza Hut** (5146 Kanan Rd., Agoura Hills, tel. 818/991–7508).

PETERSEN AUTOMOTIVE MUSEUM

Southern Californians are known for their fascination with anything automobile-related. Extravagant cars are so common here that the average Beverly Hills parking lot (valet, of course) looks more like a luxury sports-car dealership. If you want to get close to some classics without setting off a cacophony of car alarms, come to this shrine to that most prized of southern California accessories: the automobile.

With three floors of exhibits, the Petersen does its job well, offering a glimpse into California's road-faring past and a chance to ogle a large collection of prized cars, from vintage to cutting-edge. The first floor's Streetscape invites you to walk through the early days of automotive history—including a 1920s gas station and a 1940s strip mall—and actually board an old-time trolley. Upstairs, rotating galleries showcase famous Hollywood vehicles—the Flintstone mobile, to name one—as well as more contemporary hot rods and motorcycles.

KEEP IN MIND The museum was recently sold, and longtime visitors should be aware that membership no longer includes entry to such local favorites as the Natural History Museum. You'll still get some perks, however, such as a look at some rare autos during the museum's annual open house.

EATS FOR KIDS The food at fun **Ed Debevic's** (134 La Cienega Blvd., Beverly Hills, tel. 310/659–1952) is almost beside the point. The crazily clad wait staff at this '50s-style café serves burgers and other satisfying fare, and jumps up and dances about once every hour. In the ultratrendy Beverly Center, the **Hard Rock Cafe** (8600 Beverly Blvd., Beverly Hills, tel. 310/276–7605) serves burgers, fries, salads, and all the rock 'n' roll memorabilia you can stomach.

6060 Wilshire Blvd., at Fairfax Ave.

 $7 ages 13 and up, $3 children 5–12

 T–Su 10–6 (Discovery Center to 5)

323/930–CARS; www.petersen.org

3 and up

For kids, the real fun stuff is most definitely in the museum's third-floor Discovery Center, a collection of interactive gizmos that lets them unravel the science of driving and even experiment a little behind the wheel. Among activities are a giant dashboard complete with working gauges and a "truck" with age-appropriate activities. Kids love the Model T, which they can board while wearing period clothes (provided). In the Vroom Room, check out the California Highway Patrol motorcycle that emits sound effects when you take a seat. A favorite Discovery Center spot provides a test of familial cooperation. Here your brood is challenged to work together to power a model car's "combustion engine." As in a real car, pistons are activated by spark plugs (in this case, human ones). Working together and timing your footwork right will actually turn the crankshaft and make the car move.

HEY, KIDS! Not long ago, Toyota and Honda came out with the seemingly newfangled concept of a hybrid electric/gas car. But the idea is older than your grandparents. As far back as 1917, an American gentleman by the name of Woods harnessed the concept to prevent stalling on railroad tracks (cars would go from 0 to 20 on electricity and run on gas at higher speeds). The Woods Dual Power is on display at the Petersen.

PRACTICALLY PERFECT TEA

Put on the lacy frock, don the chapeau, and raise your pinky: Dressing up was made for this. Such is the fancy of taking high tea with Mary—Mary Poppins, that is—the magical nanny made famous in literature and film. Though it's not exactly the Ritz, the second-floor parlor of the Disney's Paradise Pier Hotel makes for a pleasant and child-friendly affair. Dainty music plays while mothers, grandmothers, and daughters (we're not trying to be sexist here; it's just that the overwhelming sentiment seems to be that it's just not a "guy" thing) sip tea and dish crumpets from perches in elegant settees.

Visitors to this Victorian delight will first have to make that all-important beverage decision: coffee, tea, . . . or chocolate milk? Light snacks, all served on delicate china, include scones with a variety of dainty jams, finger sandwiches (cucumber, turkey and mango, and chicken salad, among them), and pastries. Little ones can enjoy a plateful of delicacies created especially for them. Kid-specific fare includes the indispensable PB&J

KEEP IN MIND This pleasant little affair manages to be sweet without being cloying. If you aren't in the mood for the cutesy Disney version, however, there are more sophisticated (albeit more expensive) tea-totaling options available throughout the fashionable streets of Beverly Hills. (Actually, adults can request champagne at some, for an extra fee.) Two to try: the Peninsula (tel. 310/551–2888) and the Regent Beverly Wilshire (tel. 310/275–5200).

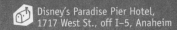
Disney's Paradise Pier Hotel,
1717 West St., off I–5, Anaheim

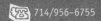 714/956–6755

 $21.95 ages 12 and up,
$13.50 children 11 and
under

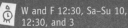 W and F 12:30, Sa–Su 10,
12:30, and 3

 3–10

as well as Mickey-shaped waffles. And of course there's plenty of tea—English breakfast, hot cinnamon spice, black cherry, and peach fruit—some in decaf versions so everyone can try them.

While you nibble, Mary appears, singing songs and sharing some of the wisdom that has made her so popular on the nanny circuit. The best part comes after the song and dance numbers, when Mary goes table to table, chatting about her days with the Banks family and dispensing advice about proper etiquette. (Don't even think about putting your elbows on the table or saying "supercalifragilisticexpialidocious" with your mouth full!) Act Two brings Mary back center stage for a song-and-soft-shoe finale. Afterwards, everyone can try on some of Ms. Poppins's elaborate garb (the big hats and boas are favorites) and pose for pictures.

HEY, KIDS! No doubt you're most familiar with Mary Poppins as a modern invention by Walt Disney. But the fabled nanny appeared long before Disneyland—in 1934, to be precise—direct from the imagination of one Pamela L. Travers. Why don't you try out some of the books?

EATS FOR KIDS If the tea's light fare doesn't fill you up, try the **PCH Grill,** on the hotel's first floor. Here grown-ups eat classy fare, while kids make their own pizza. At **Tiffy's** (1060 W. Katella Ave., tel. 714/635–1801), you can fill up on comfort food or Italian or Mexican favorites, but leave room for some home-made ice cream (try the chocolate peanut butter). Entrées start at about $6; most kids' meals run $4.

PUPPETOLIO

In the heart of Santa Monica's trendy downtown beach scene, Steve Meltzer's durable puppet show is one of those places that helps turn an average weekend day into a vacation. Bring your pre-schooler or young grade-schooler to this pleasing, informal little puppet performance, and then spend the day taking in the rest of the town's sights.

The small storefront shop hides a theater that is surprisingly cozy. Clearly, Meltzer has taken great care in its design, fashioning a comfy little spot that looks, on the inside, like a mini version of an old-time movie house.

Meltzer begins his performance by cranking up an old-fashioned Victrola and launching into a few magic tricks. David Copperfield he isn't, but his low-key rope and coin tricks are well done, and kids marvel as foreign objects magically turn up in unlikely places— such as their shoes. In the approximately one hour that follows, the puppet man introduces a handful of alter egos, such as costar Fred and musician Woodrow. A big

EATS FOR KIDS The pizza's pretty good at **Pizzarito** (1310 3rd St. Promenade, tel. 310/ 458– 9336), and you can sit outside and people-watch. **Wolfgang Puck Express** (1315 3rd St. Promenade, tel. 310/576–4770) is there, too, with particularly good sandwiches and salads.

KEEP IN MIND Reservations aren't generally required, but it's good to call ahead, as some shows fill up. Kids 8 and up can also take puppet workshops. Meltzer's setup is near the 3rd Street Promenade, where street performers (mimes, magicians, balloon artists, and assorted oddities) often appear on weekends. Bright Child (1415 4th St., tel. 310/393–4844), an expansive indoor kids playground, is also nearby.

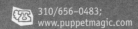

Santa Monica Puppet and Magic Center,
1255 2nd St., Santa Monica

$6.50

W 1; Sa 1, 3, and 8; Su 1 and 3

310/656-0483;
www.puppetmagic.com

3–6

highlight occurs in the middle of the show, when Meltzer produces a drawing board that has a life of its own.

Puppetolio is admittedly a bit short on polish, with puppet operations often obvious and occasionally even on the clunky side. But kids don't seem to mind, as evidenced by the giant smiles and belly laughs from the appreciative audience. In a land where impersonal, stadium-size shows are the norm, such up-close proximity to the performer is to be relished. And Meltzer's enthusiasm for his job—and his lifelong love for puppeteering—is infectious. After the show, guests are invited to tour his small workshop/museum (he makes some of his own puppets), where grownups can wax nostalgic about puppets from their youth (remember *Fireball XL5*?). His only request: look, but don't touch. There is a bit of a retail angle, as a store here does sell puppets and trinkets, but Meltzer doesn't advertise during the show, and his prices are quite reasonable.

HEY, KIDS! What's a Topo Gigio? Long before a green frog and a vain pig made headlines, this silly-voiced mouse—along with others, such as a certain top-hatted chap named Charlie McCarthy—ruled the puppet universe. Look up at the walls for photos of some of Mr. Meltzer's idols, and be sure to ask Mom and Dad if they remember the little guy named Topo and that famous phrase, "Kiss me goodnight, Eddy."

QUEEN MARY

18

Swing music from the 1930s plays as you cross the gangway onto this grande dame of ocean liners. With much of its original splendor intact, the *Queen Mary* is a step back in time, an exercise in living history. The best part is that you get all the inherent adventure of a cruise ship at sea without ever leaving port—and hence, never getting seasick.

Thanks to richly paneled hallways and original fixtures, it's easy to imagine the *Queen Mary* in her heyday. Much of the fun here—as on any cruise ship—is exploring all the nooks and crannies. Unlike a working cruise ship, however, the *Queen Mary* is completely accessible, from the engine room right up to the wheelhouse. While you tour, mingle with on-board "residents" in the form of WWII soldiers, war brides, and other passengers, all clad in clothing of the time. Be sure to stroll back to the photo gallery, where you'll find pictures of the luminaries who actually sailed on the ship, including Elizabeth Taylor, Bing Crosby, and Alfred Hitchcock.

KEEP IN MIND Ghosts and Legends is geared toward families, but special effects may be too much for youngsters. First-Class passes cover discounted admission to the *Queen Mary* and *Scorpion* (see #13), plus guided historical tours and special exhibits. Since you needn't see both vessels on the same day, why not stay overnight on the *Queen Mary* in between? Rooms run $79--$400 (cheaper rooms are small). Many original appointments remain, but modern luxuries have been added. Every Tuesday, the Queen Salon hosts free big-band dancing 12–2. Beware of the first weekend in April, however, when the Toyota Grand Prix makes getting here a bear.

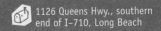
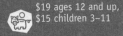

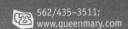

Historic exhibits here include crew quarters, preserved just as they were during the ship's sailing days. More interesting, however, are the passenger-oriented exhibits, including the barber shop, the gym, the chapel, and even a playground, all hauntingly preserved as if previous passengers were about to return. In fact, numerous on-board ghost sightings indicate they just might. The recently added Ghosts and Legends of the *Queen Mary* show (included in general admission) takes you on a tour of some of the purportedly haunted spots, including the boiler rooms and the first-class pool, areas not previously open to the public. There are also several rooms depicting the ship during its Grey Ghost days—the period during World War II when she was painted gray and used as a military transport. Hitler reportedly offered a reward worth $250,000 to the crew of any sub that could bring the *Queen Mary* down. It's a blessing to all of us that no one succeeded.

HEY, KIDS! In her day, the *Titanic* was considered the largest ship at sea, but had she stayed afloat, she would have been dwarfed by the *Queen Mary*. Launched 24 years after the *Titanic* sank, the faster *Queen Mary* could have held 3½ *Titanics* in her hull.

EATS FOR KIDS Downstairs, the **Grand Salon** (formerly the ship's first-class dining area) hosts a divine weekly Sunday brunch 10–2. The chow line at the **Sundeck Deli** looks just like what you would have found at a WWII base, but the food is better. Look for counter-service sandwiches, hot dogs, salads, and snacks—not to mention some tasty-looking pastries. Out in the Queen Mary Seaport, you'll find the type of food you'd expect at the **Queen's Barbecue** and **Market Place Pizza.** Also see eateries in the *Scorpion*.

RAGING WATERS

If you're looking to get wet, this is the place. Since its opening in 1983, this sprawling park has cooled off nearly 10 million visitors, and it's been labeled by a trade organization as one of the most popular water parks in the nation. And no wonder. In an area known for some pretty toasty temperatures, Raging Waters is indeed a great place to keep cool.

About 30 minutes east of the city, the colorful park has appealing landscaping that manages to sidestep that sterile, cement feel often characteristic of such establishments. But the big draw here is the size (50 acres) and the scope (more than 50 attractions). There's something for everybody, and new attractions are added to the park annually.

Newer additions include El Niño, a flume that pays homage to California's notorious weather event. Daredevils will want to head straight for the Dropout, one of those fall-off-the-

HEY, KIDS!
The best part of the Wedge, which mimics skateboarding on a street course's half pipe, is picking whether to ride forwards, backwards, or sideways. The extreme effect is so inspiring, one couple got married at the top and then sped down to the bottom (honest).

KEEP IN MIND Raging Waters alters its hours to keep up with daylight; in midsummer, you'll be able to keep sliding well into the evening. And there are other ways to get the most for your money, so be sure to ask about any promotions. If you plan to come often, check out the reasonably priced 20-visit and annual passes.

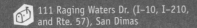
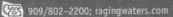

side-of-the-earth contraptions that you'll find either exhilarating or terrifying. Cross your arms and legs and plunge down a seven-story drop in roughly four seconds. (Note: one-piece bathing suits are recommended.) For anyone keeping score, there are also a couple of record-setters here, such as High EXtreme, at 100 feet tall (200 steps up), the tallest head-first slide in the world. Other thrill attractions have characteristically ominous names, such as the Dark Hole, the Vortex, and the Bermuda Triangle.

Although even the smallest children can turn inexplicably fearless here, less-adventurous tots (and their grown-ups) will find plenty that includes them in the fun. The Kids Kingdom actually looks like a typical neighborhood playground, only with sprinklers, sprays, and mini tube slides. Families can also have lots of fun climbing and sliding at both the Volcano FantaSea, a slide and splash area inside a "volcanic mountain," and Splash Island Adventure, a five-story aquatic climbing sculpture.

EATS FOR KIDS There are plenty of places to eat inside the park, including the **Pizza Place** and **Burgers 'n' Fries.** Outside in the cute little town of San Dimas, you'll find a number of comfortable restaurants, including **Applebee's Neighborhood Grill & Bar** (674 W. Arrow Hwy., tel. 909/ 394–7600), which serves burgers, sandwiches, salads, and ribs.

RIPLEY'S BELIEVE IT OR NOT! MUSEUM

If you've ever wondered about eight-legged pigs and two-headed cows, Ripley's is for you. Astounding, unbelievable, and more than occasionally a little gross, Ripley's is also a ton of fun, amounting to the museum equivalent of a car wreck in that you just can't keep from looking.

Across the street from the Movieland Wax Museum (*see* #30)—Ripley's companion museum, operated by the same company—Ripley's "Odditorium" contains unusual wonders of modern civilization. Consider the elaborate sculpture of DaVinci's *Last Supper*, carved out of 240 pieces of white bread. There's also a wax likeness of Liu Ch'ung, who was born with two pupils in each eye—one of those gross entries. Lest you think the museum is simply a tribute to weirdness (although there is a lot of that), it also has some fascinating tidbits about nature that fall under the category of "education." Your children can learn that grasshoppers have five eyes and that caterpillars possess an unexpectedly large muscle mass. The museum itself even has some rather interesting lore

KEEP IN MIND Combining visits to Ripley's and Movieland will get you a discount at the ticket office, but it's best done over a couple of days. You'll have to use half of your pass the day you buy it, but the companion ticket is good indefinitely. Both museums are open year-round, with crowds most likely during school breaks. Even so, peak-season visits can be surprisingly uncrowded and make for a perfect air-conditioned diversion.

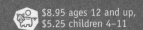 7850 Beach Blvd., Buena Park

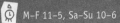 $8.95 ages 12 and up, $5.25 children 4–11

M–F 11–5, Sa–Su 10–6

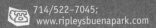 714/522–7045; www.ripleysbuenapark.com

 All ages

attached to it. Modern legend has it that women who have touched the African Fertility Totems, which circulate among the nation's Ripley museums, have soon after become pregnant (parents, take this as a warning).

Visionary Mr. Ripley, a wax figure of whom stands guard in the front lobby, makes for pretty entertaining reading, too. The nondrinking, nonsmoking, eccentric bachelor cartoonist, who died in 1949, was an oddity in and of himself.

While many consider Movieland and Ripley's to be complementary experiences, if you're doing both in one day, you may want to leave more time for the latter. Even young children seem to find the outrageous displays here curious, leading to unusually long attention spans—perhaps the biggest "Believe It or Not" of all.

HEY, KIDS! Want to become a conductor—not of a symphony or even of a train, but of electricity? Touch a knob and the metal post on the Human Conductor exhibit, and the radio begins to play. The gadget works because you complete an electrical circuit.

EATS FOR KIDS You'll find a little bit of everything—Tex-Mex food, hot dogs, ribs, sandwiches, and salad—at **Spoons Grill and Bar** (7801 Beach Blvd., tel. 714/523–1460). Kids eat free with a paying adult every Tuesday night. For entertainment, try **Medieval Times Dinner & Tournament** (7662 Beach Blvd., tel. 714/521–4740) or **Wild Bill's** (7600 Beach Blvd., tel. 714/522–6414), both of which have theme performances as well as plentiful food. Also see Movieland Wax Museum.

SANTA ANA ZOO AT PRENTICE PARK

Many people like this pleasing zoo in the heart of Orange County because it's small and easily walkable. Think of it as having the Goldilocks seal of approval; it's not too big, not too small, but "just right," with just enough surprises to entertain all members of the family without exhausting them. The zoo's 8-acre size will particularly appeal to you if you're pushing a stroller or leading an unsteady toddler. The zoo has also taken little ones' wandering attention spans to heart, providing a good-size playground at the entrance and a good rock-climbing spot at the zoo's center.

But the animals are most definitely the real stars. Emus, rheas (resembling small ostriches), monkeys, wallabies, and a family of capybara—the world's largest rodent for anyone who's interested—are among the zoo's 250 animals on display. Most are visible in their habitats, but there are a couple of roosters that amuse and surprise visitors by walking around (and crowing) freely. The striking Colors of the Amazon exhibit, a large and well-landscaped walk-through aviary, features streams, ponds, and a rain forest.

EATS FOR KIDS The on-site **La Perla del Amazonas** (tel. 714/543–5991) serves surprisingly tasty foods, including Mexican and American favorites. Outside the zoo, **Rutabegorz** (158 W. Main St., Tustin, tel. 714/731–9807) has soups, salads, pastas, and vegetarian entrées, as well as some great desserts.

HEY, KIDS! How many languages do you think the average pig speaks? According to the Sounds Heard 'Round the World chart in the children's zoo, though a pig in this country says "Oink," its Japanese counterparts snort "ink, ink, bubu." OK, so they're not exactly perfect interpretations. The chart won't tell you what pigs sound like in Pig Latin—you'll have to figure that out for yourself—but you can check out many more wild translations. Does that mean that if an animal moves to another country, it has to become bilingual to speak to its new furry friends?

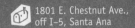 1801 E. Chestnut Ave., off I-5, Santa Ana

 714/835-7484; www.santaanazoo.org

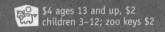 $4 ages 13 and up, $2 children 3–12; zoo keys $2

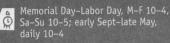 Memorial Day–Labor Day, M–F 10–4, Sa–Su 10–5; early Sept–late May, daily 10–4

 All ages

Take heed when entering: The rain forest is authentic right down to the showers. If you happen to enter during one of the manmade downpours (12:30 and 3:30, but only on the hottest summer days), count on getting very wet.

Your kids can get an extra kick out of some exhibits by using a Zoo Key, available at the park entrance. Keys inserted into designated boxes by some exhibits will yield a bit of information about that animal as well as an accompanying song.

In addition to the main exhibits, there's a good-size children's zoo, where you'll find the usual suspects—sheep, pigs, goats, and even some snakes (the latter, thankfully, in glass cases). Though the zoo's wide paths are mostly paved, the children's zoo has dirt roads—ostensibly to go along with the Old McDonald's Farm feel of the red barnyard structures—making it, oddly, the hardest place to push a stroller.

KEEP IN MIND A favorite feature at the zoo is the Zoofari Express, a scale-model train that will cost you $1 to ride. The train runs Friday, Saturday, and Sunday from 11 to 3. A bit of trivia: If the train looks familiar, it probably is; the entire set (engine to caboose) was relocated from the now-defunct Santa's Village in the San Bernardino Mountains.

SATWIWA

hildren expecting movie-variety Indians at this Native American cultural education center are in for a surprise. The focus at Satwiwa is on modern Native American culture. "People expect to see us in 500-year-old feathers," explains a Satwiwa park ranger. "Here, they get a rare chance to come face-to-face with contemporary Indian people in what may be the only place they get to do that."

Located in the heart of the Santa Monica Mountains, the Satwiwa center sits on a lovely expanse of land with its roots in Chumash history (the name Satwiwa—which means "the bluffs"—was that of a nearby village long ago). Though you can hike the trails here anytime and visit the culture center the whole weekend, the time to come is on the one day each weekend when you can visit with one of the Native American hosts (seasonal schedule; call for details). In addition to enthusiastically discussing their culture and answering questions on the subject, these volunteers (representing all the Pan American people) demonstrate

KEEP IN MIND Check the schedule beforehand to catch a Native American host, especially Charlie Cooke, a Chumash chief and well-loved guide, who draws huge crowds for his four annual walks. You can also call or check the Web site for information on all Santa Monica Mountains parks. Adventurous hikers might like the 70 miles of trails at the adjoining Point Mugu State Park, where trails tend to be steep and rugged—appropriate for older kids. Check with park rangers before setting out. For other Native American explorations, consider the Chumash Interpretive Center (3290 Lang Ranch Pkwy., Thousand Oaks, tel. 805/492–8076).

Lynn Rd. and Via Goleta, Newbury Park

 Free

  Daily 8–sunset, culture center Sa–Su 9–5

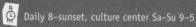 805/370–2301; www.nps.gov/samo

5 and up

such crafts as beading, basket weaving, and rug making, occasionally inviting children to participate. One day, for example, an affable Creek Seminole woman named Jane told legends of her culture and demonstrated the art of making ceremonial Ribbon Shirts, the garb commonly worn during powwows. The center occasionally features Native American dancers and storytellers, and powwows are planned for the future. If you're not lucky enough to happen upon one of these majestic pageants in person, you can watch a video. Inside, exhibits and books depict past and present Native American life.

Satwiwa's open terrain makes for some scenic hiking, and easy-to-manage trails traverse the area. The best hike for kids is the Satwiwa Loop Trail, a 1½-mile round-trip that takes you past a windmill and along an overlook of Satwiwa.

EATS FOR KIDS
A few minutes away, catch some fish-and-chips at the **Fresh Catch** (2110B Newbury Rd., tel. 805/376–9666). **Lamppost Pizza** (2160A Newbury Rd., tel. 805/499–0303) serves a tasty version of the Italian favorite.

GETTING THERE Take U.S. 101 to Lynn Road south; travel 5¼ miles, and turn left on Via Goleta, the park's main entrance road. (Note: Via Goleta is easy to miss; if you pass the Dos Vientos housing development on your right, you've gone too far.) The large main parking lot is the last one, about ¾ mile down the Via Goleta. If you park in an earlier lot, you'll have a long walk. The Satwiwa site is about ¼ mile from the lot.

SCORPION

Kids are generally fascinated by anything that floats, so imagine what they'll think of a vessel that travels underwater. The *Scorpion*, an actual Soviet submarine moored next to the *Queen Mary* (*see* #18; discounted combination tickets available), provides a look at this incredible method of aquatic travel. Though a far cry from Captain Nemo, this black Cold War craft (commissioned in 1972) nevertheless inspires more than a few exclamations of "cool!"

You start with a bit of submarine history via an orientation film. While you do learn about the vehicle's size (300 feet long), speed, and capacity, don't expect a serious scientific study. This film is so hokey that it's actually entertaining.

Still, it's the submarine itself that's the focal point. The entire interior is open, and you can pass through all seven compartments, examining the mechanics and weaponry (one disarmed torpedo remains of the 16 nuclear-tipped torpedoes once on board) as well

KEEP IN MIND Be warned: Steep ladders require good shoes (no heels). A crowded day may bother you if you're claustrophobic. The vessel occasionally sways, so beware if you're prone to seasickness. Finally, think twice about coming the first weekend in April, when the Toyota Grand Prix makes getting here hard.

EATS FOR KIDS Eating spots at the adjacent Queen Mary Seaport include the **Londontowne Deli and Bakery;** get takeout and grab one of the tables spread around the seaport. **Shoreline Village** (401–435 Shoreline Dr.), a quaint retail hamlet that's also good for biking, has **Tugboat Pete's** (tel. 562/436–4919), for burgers or barbecue sandwiches on the go, and the scenic **Parker's Lighthouse** (435 Shoreline Dr., tel. 562/432–6500). Also see the *Queen Mary.*

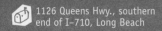 1126 Queens Hwy., southern
end of I-710, Long Beach

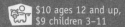 $10 ages 12 and up,
$9 children 3–11

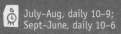 July–Aug, daily 10–9;
Sept–June, daily 10–6

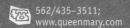 562/435-3511;
www.queenmary.com

 5 and up

as where the crew ate, slept, worked, and kept secret documents. There's even a working periscope. A chirpy Russian-accented voice prompts you from one compartment to the next, dispensing factoids, such as that the vessel has only two bathrooms and one shower (for 78 men!), that its boardroom doubled as its operating theater, and that sailors didn't wash dirty sheets—they just threw them away. (Is it any wonder the Soviet Union no longer exists?) Though the sub technically works, the instruments have been deactivated, so children can push, pull, and turn wheels without doing damage. Of course, don't try to figure out what the gadgets are for; notations are in Russian. An actual former Soviet naval officer is often on hand to answer questions.

Most striking are the accommodations: A vast luxury liner it isn't. In fact, despite its exterior size, the inside is remarkably cramped. Although there's generally room for tourists to move around—with only a few spots where you'll have to suck in your gut to pass someone—it's hard to imagine a crew of 78 holed up in here for months at a time.

HEY, KIDS! It wasn't enough to hunker down with 77 other crew-mates. Submarine officers routinely shared their compartments with cats, who not only served as companions but also helped control the onboard rat population, a significant undersea problem. If you see Igor Kolosov—an actual veteran of a Russian sub who is frequently aboard answering questions—ask about other stories of sub life.

SIX FLAGS MAGIC MOUNTAIN

Kids who like their rides scary—terrifying, actually—will find unparalleled excitement here. If Disneyland has introduced your children to theme parks, this is where they earn their stripes for bravery, surviving a mind-boggling collection of loops, drops, and yes, even, bungee jumps (or a reasonable approximation) on their way to one of the ultimate thrill experiences.

That Magic Mountain is tops in constitution testers (everything here is the "tallest, fastest" something) has been cemented with the addition of Déjà Vu and the ominously titled X. The latter's description states that "riders will plummet 200 feet to the ground—head first, face down." Sound like fun? Then hop on one of the other looping, contorting devices, including Flashback, Viper (an enormous looping coaster), Superman the Escape (with a 41-story incline at 100 mph), and Riddler's Revenge (a fast, stand-up ride). Riders may think they're having all the fun, but spectators get thrills, too, except, perhaps, while watching loved ones drop 150 feet on Dive Devil. ("Watching her do it is thrill enough for me," quipped

KEEP IN MIND Like many other amusement parks, Magic Mountain is most crowded in the summer. Families who visit after Labor Day may get the place virtually to themselves, as many people are unaware that it, unlike its next-door neighbor and sister, Six Flags Hurricane Harbor water park (26101 Magic Mountain Pkwy., tel. 661/255–4111), is a year-round operation. During the summer, ask about discounted Magic Mountain/Hurricane Harbor combo admission, and look for occasional discounts available through fast-food chains and on soft-drink containers.

 26101 Magic Mountain Pkwy., off I-5, Valencia

 818/367-5965 from Los Angeles area, 661/255-4100 elsewhere; www.sixflags.com

 $42.99 49" and up, $21.50 48" and under

 Late Mar–June, Su–Th 10–8, F–Sa 10–10; July–Labor Day, Su–Th 10–10, F–Sa 10–12; early Sept–Oct, F–Su 10–6; Nov–mid-Mar, Sa–Su 10–6

 2 and up

the boyfriend of one diver.) Dive Devil is so popular that you'll have to make reservations upon arrival and pay an extra fee ($28–$48).

Not all the rides are so extreme; the less adventurous can find happiness at the Grand Carousel, Log Jammer flume ride, or Bugs Bunny World. The addition of Goliath Jr., a miniature version of the big kids' ride, brings the number of kid-size coasters to two (the other is Canyon Blaster). Except for Goliath Jr., there are no height maximums for the kiddie rides, so parents can ride along.

Still, since visitors pay primarily for thrills (not to mention the park's liability insurance), if you're toting only smaller children, you're probably best off at a tamer, less expensive establishment (*see* Adventure City). Even if the prospect of abject terror doesn't detour your young thrill seekers, the height requirements (most grown-up rides have a 48" minimum) might.

HEY, KIDS! Your parents may put the kibosh on Dive Devil (even if the 48" minimum height doesn't), but you can still feel like you're defying gravity on rides like Superman and Freefall, both of which feature significant drops that create a momentary feeling of weightlessness. Hold onto your stomachs.

EATS FOR KIDS As at any theme park, there's no shortage of eats at Magic Mountain. Two good ones to try: the **Pizza Vector** (Gotham City) and the **Mooseburger Lodge** (High Sierra Territory). The latter tends to get crowded around noon, but you can make lunch and dinner reservations at the restaurant when you get to the park. Cuisines are basically self-explanatory.

SOLSTICE CANYON

Of all the colorful hikes in the Santa Monica Mountains, this is my family's favorite. Shady and lush with ocean breezes providing cool relief on even the hottest southern California days, the Solstice Canyon Trail route is scenic hiking at its best, a place where wide pathways and flat terrain make it possible for even young children to put on their sneaks and enjoy. A wonderful getaway from the L.A. hubbub, it might as easily be called Solace Canyon.

An old road takes you along a maze of gurgling creeks. Though you may be tempted to stray into them, rangers caution against it; besides, even on the hottest days, the water's c-c-c-cold, and there's lots of poison oak down there. Listen along the way for the rustling sounds of wildlife, including tiny lizards that regularly scurry across your path. There are plenty of tadpoles around, too, as well as scads of colorful butterflies.

GETTING THERE Take the Pacific Coast Highway to Corral Canyon Road north. Travel ¼ mile to the park entrance, on the left, marked by an inconspicuous white gate with a sign. If you make a hard right turn and start winding through the mountains, you've gone too far.

KEEP IN MIND Though the terrain is largely flat, only about ⅔ of the route is paved. After that, strollers become tough to push. Your safest bet is to don the old backpack carrier. If you do, you'll want to take the right (stream-side) fork near the end of the trail, as the left side is more challenging with added weight on your back. Call the Visitor Center to learn about other trails, and beware of weekend crowds, which can make parking difficult, if not impossible. If you do come on a Saturday or Sunday, arrive by 9:30. Current plans call for the park to be shut down temporarily for remodeling; call for a schedule.

For many people, the trip's highlight is Tropical Terrace, the remains of a mansion burned down in the 1980s. Though the home's 1950s construction makes it less than antique, there's nevertheless something otherworldly and ethereal about it (think *Planet of the Apes*). While much of it is gone, stone structures such as patios, fireplaces, and a few rooms remain—all overgrown with tropical greenery, hence the name—making for some neat stomping grounds to explore.

If you're speeding along, you can probably travel the entire 2.1-mile Solstice Canyon Trail in about an hour. But this is definitely a "stop and smell the roses" tour—or at least a "stop and watch the lizards" tour. Your kids will no doubt want to linger around waterfalls and rocky areas, and the Tropical Terrace makes a serene spot for a family picnic. Other Solstice Canyon trails, such as the Deer Valley Loop and the Rising Sun paths, are a good deal more challenging, taking you right through the mountains and occasionally requiring you to push aside brush to get through. They are best for experienced hiking families with preteens and teens.

EATS FOR KIDS An obvious choice is to pack a picnic. However, if you're tired of making sandwiches, you can dine overlooking the beach at **Malibu Fish and Seafood** (25653 Pacific Coast Hwy., tel. 310/456–3430), known among locals for its really fresh and reasonably priced seafood, from fish-and-chips to swordfish. Supposedly, nothing is more than two hours old. If you'd like to give the kids more options than just those from the sea, try the **Marmalade Café** (3894 Cross Creek Rd., tel. 310/317–4242), which serves soups, salads, pastas, and lots more.

SPEEDZONE

Young adolescents pining for their licenses can see how their driving prowess stacks up against Mom's and Dad's at this miniature raceway built for amateurs. A veritable speed-demon fantasy land, the 12-acre park features four tracks—the Top Eliminator, Grand Prix, Slick Trax, and Turbo Track—on which you can career and compete in scaled-down versions of the race cars you see on TV.

Experiences range from tame to extreme. The most exhilarating, Top Eliminator, is truly of the "Peel Your Eyelids off Your Forehead" variety the brochures purport it to be. Drivers in 300-hp dragsters get to control acceleration and shifting—no steering necessary, as Top Eliminator cars run on a metal rail—and race five other drivers down a 140-yard stretch. Cars go from 0 to 70 in three seconds. The short but memorable experience is gloriously authentic: Christmas Tree lights start you out of the gate, and a force equivalent to three g's throws you back in your seat. Braking, thankfully, is done by computer at the finish line.

KEEP IN MIND Anyone at least 5' tall is automatically authorized to go on three of the tracks, but you'll need a driver's license for the Grand Prix. Children under 13 who are at least 36" tall can ride as a passenger with an adult driver on Turbo Track. For information about frequent promotions and about the Adrenaline Club—its membership card gives you discounts on future visits—check out the Web site.

17871 Castleton St.,
off Rte. 60, City of Industry

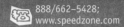
888/662-5428;
www.speedzone.com

Su–Th 11 AM–12 AM, F–Sa 11 AM–1 AM

$3 and up, avg $15/person

13 and up

Other SpeedZone tracks focus more on skill than sheer adrenaline. In Slick Trax, for example, drivers need to master the art of cornering and braking through turns in order to maneuver the ultraslippery road surface without skidding. All tracks have electronic scoreboards to display times, and you and your children can take home printouts of your accomplishments.

Since professional race drivers consulted on the design, SpeedZone feels like the real thing or, as the brochures again boast, "The closest thing to professional racing offered to the public." For safety, cars have been designed low and wide to avoid tipping. In the event of a problem, all vehicles can be instantly shut down from a central control station. Some tracks charge by the minute and others by the lap. There is also an extensive arcade, as well as two miniature golf courses in case your need for speed abates.

HEY, KIDS! Think you go fast here? Top Eliminator's dragsters peel out and reach top speeds of 70 mph. But that's nothing next to the pros. Real drag racers can reach speeds upwards of 200 mph.

EATS FOR KIDS Alongside the arcade, the **SpeedZone Café** offers full-service meals—burgers, fries, etc.—as well as snacks. Outside the park, you can continue the car theme at **Frisco's Car Hop Diner** (18065 Gale Ave., tel. 626/913-3663). It features roller-skating waitresses, classic-car booths, and diner favorites.

TELEVISION TAPINGS

Lots of Los Angeles attractions take you behind the scenes to reveal how shows are produced, but only one activity enables you to actually see a production take shape: the studio-audience experience. Virtually every live-studio-audience show is up for grabs, including *All That* and other popular fare. Though viewers may feel privileged to garner a seat, the producer/audience relationship is a symbiotic one. Tourists can watch their favorite stars, while producers get bodies to supply those all-important audience reactions.

Audience members find a festive, party atmosphere thanks largely to comedians who act as congenial masters of ceremonies between takes. You also get a firsthand look at outtakes you just might see later on one of those myriad bloopers shows. The downside can be the time required and tedium that sets in if take after take of the same scene is required. In fact, don't be surprised if a ½-hour sitcom takes several hours to complete.

HEY, KIDS!
Entertainment at TV tapings isn't limited to what's going on on stage. Funny men and women are generally on hand to keep you whooping it up between takes. Keep your eyes peeled; you may be in the presence of a future comedy star. And be prepared to clap—a lot!

KEEP IN MIND Another good ticket service is www.tvtix.com. For same-day (weekday), pot-luck tickets, try Universal Studios CityWalk (100 Universal City Plaza, Universal City, tel. 818/622–3801). Going through Paramount (5555 Melrose Ave., tel. 323/956–1777) has the advantage that reservations are taken a maximum of five days out. For the *Tonight Show with Jay Leno*, contact NBC (3000 W. Alameda Ave., Burbank 91523, tel. 818/840–3537) or get to the studio at 8 AM, when a limited number of same-day passes are distributed. For all shows, arrive at least 90 minutes before taping. Productions overbook to ensure plenty of guffawers, and you *can* be bumped.

Call for studio addresses

Free

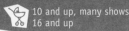

Hrs vary; most shows tape M–F evening

818/753–3470 Audiences Unlimited;
www.tvtickets.com

10 and up, many shows
16 and up

The most easily accessible passes are likely to be for new shows and pilots, for which producers need to build audiences. That could mean watching something wonderful or something dreadful—after all, even *The Michael Richards Show* had an audience . . . once. In most cases, you have to request tickets at least a few weeks ahead, and really hot shows sometimes require planning months in advance. A good way to obtain tickets is through Audiences Unlimited, a clearinghouse for TV tapings. Tickets are available by phone, mail, and e-mail (call or see its Web site for instructions). When making your all-important booking, be sure to ask about age requirements, as they vary from show to show. Audiences Unlimited makes it easy to "shop" by posting minimum ages for each program on its Web site. Most shows' producers like their audiences on the older side (roughly 16 and up), not just for the production's content, but also for the shenanigans that ensue between takes. Elementary schoolers, however, aren't totally left out; some shows (particularly those associated with kids' networks) occasionally welcome guests as young as 8.

EATS FOR KIDS If you're attending an evening taping, you'll want to grab a bite first. You'll find Korean barbecue at **Woo Lae Oak** (623 S. Western Ave., tel. 213/384–2244), where individual hibachi grills enable you to cook your own dinner at your table (unless, of course, you do enough cooking at home). If your taping takes you to the Burbank area, try the **Hard Rock Cafe** (1000 Universal Center Dr., Universal City, tel. 818/622–7625), where atmosphere and people-watching overshadow the adequate salads, burgers, and sandwiches.

TRAVEL TOWN MUSEUM

8

In a region known for big-bang attractions, this endearing, low-key spot—a shrine to all things railroad—might well be called the little museum that could. A retirement home for long-since-derailed vintage locomotives, the unassuming gem is a veritable train heaven, a place where kids can climb aboard, daydream, and explore.

With a cast of several dozen old stalwarts (40 at last count), the collection is comprehensive; look for everything from an 1880 Southern Pacific locomotive to a 1910 Western Pacific caboose, not to mention turn-of-the-20th-century Los Angeles railway trolleys and an 1880 horse-drawn railway car. The 1864 Stockton Terminal & Eastern No. 1 is a kid favorite because of its red and black design that seems to have come out of a story. The number and configuration of trains changes, so you'll have to look around for what you want to see.

Other novelties include wagons and automobiles significant in Los Angeles history and an exhibit building with antique fire engines and related equipment.

KEEP IN MIND Though you can climb inside some vehicles, you'll spend much time milling about outdoors, so you'll want to pick a day when heat or rain isn't overwhelming. You can also take a ride through the outlying grounds on the scale-model Griffith Park Southern Railroad (Los Feliz Blvd. and Riverside Dr., tel. 323/664–6788). Two trains travel a mile of track past the park's scenery and attractions. A fixture here since 1931, the Griffith Park Merry-Go-Round (tel. 323/665–3051), in the center of the park, is open weekends year-round, weekdays in summer.

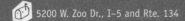 5200 W. Zoo Dr., I–5 and Rte. 134

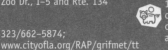 323/662–5874;
www.cityofla.org/RAP/grifmet/tt

Free; train ride $2 ages
14 and up, $1.50
children 19 mth–13 yr;
caboose ride, donations
accepted

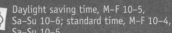 Daylight saving time, M–F 10–5,
Sa–Su 10–6; standard time, M–F 10–4,
Sa–Su 10–5

 3–8

You can mill about the entire yard, weaving in and out of these iron maidens that stand idle on antique tracks. Some of the collection can be climbed aboard; others are there just to look at. Although the antique behemoths will no doubt inspire fantasies of great train robbers making dramatic escapes across the train tops, your kids will have to imagine it all from the ground, as no one is allowed to scale the outside or roofs of the trains. The equipment is stationary except for the charming ride-on train that chugs around the park's perimeter—directed by a classically dressed conductor, of course—and a restored circa-1941 diesel engine that hooks up to two cabooses each month (usually the first and third weekends) and takes passengers on a few-minute trip along the museum's length. An elaborate scale-model train layout is generally on display on weekends.

HEY, KIDS! How much do you suppose the big engines weigh? Consider it in terms of elephants. The average African elephant (the big guys with the floppy ears) weighs in at about 7 tons. The Stockton Terminal & Eastern No. 1 weighs in at about 33 tons—the equivalent of almost five elephants!

EATS FOR KIDS For on-the-spot eats, there's the **Dining Car** (tel. 323/662–9840), a window-service snack shack whose menu includes hot dogs, chicken, pizza, and snacks. **California Pizza Kitchen** (101 N. Brand Blvd., Glendale, tel. 818/507–1558) offers the franchise's tasty pizzas and salads within about a 10-minute drive.

UNIVERSAL STUDIOS HOLLYWOOD

7

If you can't actually be in the movies, the next best thing is to "ride" them—precisely the premise of this theme park built around a working film studio. A conglomeration of flight simulators, special-effects encounters, thrill rides, and soundstages, Universal is an extreme version of Disneyland—a place where fantasy becomes a very vivid reality.

Attractions incorporate themes from popular movies, some worth riding for the scenery, such as the "bike ride" through E.T.'s homeland (E.T. Adventure), others for thrills. If you're a flight-simulator fan, you won't want to miss *Back to the Future*—The Ride, an unparalleled jostle through time in Doc Brown's trademark DeLorean. Special-effects enthusiasts will be impressed by *Backdraft,* in which you actually feel flames, and *WaterWorld*—A Live Sea War Spectacular.

Many of the park's trademark elements (Jaws, King Kong, Earthquake—The Big One) can be found on Universal's back-lot tram tour. Though the gimmicks make for a good time,

EATS FOR KIDS Universal has food carts, restaurants, and cafeterias. For retro, try **Mel's Diner,** a '50s-style hop. While you dry out from Jurassic Park, enjoy dino-size burgers and chicken at **Jurassic Cove.**

HEY, KIDS! Even on a hot California day, the Blast Zone is totally cool. Based on some of Nickelodeon's popular TV fare (*SpongeBob SquarePants, The Wild Thornberrys*), the place is filled with buckets, hoses (called Blasters), and various other contraptions designed to get you and your loved ones soaked. Cowabunga!

 100 Universal City Plaza.,
off U.S. 101, Universal City

 $43 ages 12 and up,
$33 children 3–11

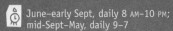 June–early Sept, daily 8 AM–10 PM;
mid-Sept–May, daily 9–7

 818/622-3801, 800/UNIVERSAL;
www.universalstudioshollywood.com

6 and up

having to see them combined into one package can make the tour feel excruciatingly long—particularly with young children. However, since some of the effects on the tour (such as the Mummy) are pretty intense, you might want to rethink taking little ones anyway. *Jurassic Park*—The Ride, a flume trip down an 85-foot drop, is a hoot if you like this sort of thing. But be warned that you're best off doing this one late in the day, as you won't get wet, but rather completely soaked. (Disposable raincoats—a particularly good idea in winter—are sold at the ride's entrance.) *Terminator 2:* 3D, a live-action, 3-D film/special-effects gig, definitely packs a punch. Fans of *The Mummy Returns* can immerse themselves in the film via the park's ominously named Chamber of Doom.

Universal also has a couple of shows worth seeing, most notably Nickelodeon's *Rug Rats Magic Adventure*. Unlike previous Nick shows, there's no slime here. And any little kids you've brought are sure to love the *Animal Planet Live,* with furry (and too-cute) performers aplenty.

KEEP IN MIND The shows at Universal are for all ages, but there isn't much in the ride department for the under-7 set. In the shoe department, nix the sandals here. The upper-lot/lower-lot layout makes for a lot of walking. Before leaving Universal City, make sure to get an eyeful of the Universal Studios CityWalk, which contains restaurant/clubs, unusual shops, and some pretty interesting people-watching.

UPPER NEWPORT BAY ECOLOGICAL RESERVE

I f ever there was an antidote to the Los Angeles hustle and bustle, this ecological reserve is it. A rare find amid the beach scenes and expensive homes of most southern California coastal communities, Upper Newport Bay, an estuary an hour south of the city, can really make you and your family feel you've gotten away from it all.

The most popular way to enjoy the area is by boat—specifically canoes and kayaks. Many Saturday mornings, the reserve's volunteer naturalists lead visitors on scenic canoe paddles around the area. Alternatively, you can book a Sunday kayak tour through Resort Watersports at the Newport Dunes Resort (tel. 949/729-1150); these trips cost more but start later in the morning and can accommodate children as young as 2. Either way, tours run about two hours, with roughly 2–3 miles' worth of paddling.

The bay is home to large, colorful, and, in many cases, rare birds, which you can spy while enjoying this serene wetland. (Surprisingly, spring, fall, and winter scenery is best.) Birds

KEEP IN MIND On request, the canoe tour fee will cover California Wildlife Campaign membership, entitling you to a year's unlimited canoe trips and half-price kayak trips. Rangers suggest reserving three weeks ahead for canoe tours. Though Resort Watersports is mostly open weekends only, you can arrange for boat rental at any time by calling during operating hours. Contact Amigos de Bolsa Chica (Warner Ave. and Pacific Coast Hwy., Huntington Beach, tel. 714/840-1575) about walking tours of the Bolsa Chica Ecological Reserve.

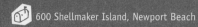 600 Shellmaker Island, Newport Beach

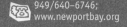 949/640-6746;
www.newportbay.org

 Free; canoe tour $13 ages 16 and up, children free; kayak tour $20 ages 13 and up, $15 children 2-12

 Daily 8-sunset, canoe tour Sa 8:30, kayak tour Su 10

 Canoe tour 7 and up, kayak tour 2 and up

to look for include members of the heron family, such as great blue herons and snowy egrets, as well as the occasional pelican. Many of these local residents are large—about 3' tall with wing spans up to 6'—making them particularly captivating to young children. Once in a great while, you might even spy a sea lion.

If you'd prefer to go it alone, the adjacent Newport Dunes Resort rents kayaks hourly as well; you'll just have to stay off the islands and in the boat. (The resort [tel. 949/729-3863] also has a lagoon to swim in and watercraft and bicycles for rent.) Devout landlubbers can enjoy the scenery via the ecological reserve's free guided nature walks, on the first and third Saturdays of every month, or by taking a self-guided walk any day.

Both reserve and resort offer other children's activities, including summer evening camp fires.

HEY, KIDS! Look for the dramatic fishing style of ospreys, which swoop down to the water and grab fish in their talons. They typically nest in eucalyptus trees but are hard to spot. Their nests, however, can often easily be seen in trees and on buoys in channels. To spot baby birds, look in late spring.

EATS FOR KIDS The Newport Dunes Resort's **Back Bay Cafe** (1131 Back Bay Dr., tel. 949/729-1144) serves hamburgers, sandwiches, and a children's menu. Not far from the reserve, **Joe's Crab Shack** (2607 W. Pacific Coast Hwy., tel. 949/650-1818) serves fresh seafood bay-side; kids like the pizza, chicken fingers, and hot dogs.

VANS SKATEPARK

Snag your board, Ollie up to the handrail, grab Indy, land, and ride 50-50 down the rail. (In English, for you parents, that's roughly translated as riding straight down a handrail.) This place is heaven on wheels.

Vans, known worldwide as a leading skateboard equipment manufacturer, has provided a whiz-bang haven for local extreme sporters. The mammoth, 46,000-square-foot mecca stood briefly as the world's largest—that is until Vans opened a few bigger, even fancier ones in other parts of the country. Nevertheless, enthusiasts and pros (both boarders and in-line skaters) continue to scope the place out in droves. On any given day, your kids may be Ollie-ing around with the likes of Omar Hassan, Steve Caballero, or Jen O'Brien (you may not know who they are, but your kids probably will).

In addition to banks and ledges, boarders will find a bit of nostalgia in the form of the Combi Pool, an exact replica of the world-famous Upland Pipeline Skatepark

HEY, KIDS!
Look for details about the Vans Amateur World Championships of Skateboarding, an elite event held at the park annually. Admission is free. Though the park is emptiest during school hours, don't even think about cutting class to get in; Vans does a check on all school-age kids.

KEEP IN MIND All boarders/skaters are required to wear helmets, knee pads, and elbow pads. Wrist guards are optional. Safety equipment can be rented on-site; other equipment is BYOB (bring your own boards and blades). If you're a serious skater, consider an annual membership—generally $50, but there are occasional sales—which cuts your per-session price; savings start to add up if you go once a month or more.

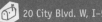 20 City Blvd. W, I-5 and Rte. 22, Orange

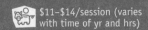 $11–$14/session (varies with time of yr and hrs)

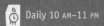 Daily 10 AM–11 PM

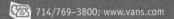 714/769–3800; www.vans.com

 4 and up

course that closed in the 1980s. The Combi is the most technical of Vans's three pools, notable for being in-ground, a superior (and more expensive) alternative to the above-ground pools found at most public parks. To boot, there's an 80-foot-wide vertical ramp and 18,000-square-foot street course. If you're up for learning a new trick or two, ask about free lessons (weekdays 4:45–6:45), which are included in the two-hour session fee. Lesson availability can change, so call ahead. The place even has a designated peewee area for budding roller enthusiasts of all ages (for practical purposes, we're talking from about age 4); bring your own skates if you plan on accompanying your kids, as no pedestrians are allowed on the floor.

Vicarious thrill seekers (and the simply faint of heart) can look out over the action (for free) from the 6,000-square-foot mezzanine. From there, you can feel safe in the knowledge that the skate areas are patrolled by a competent, first-aid-trained staff.

EATS FOR KIDS The Block at Orange, the mall that is home to Vans, houses a typically vast number of fast-food and snack haunts ranging from **Jody Maroni's Sausage Kingdom** to **Starbucks Café.** If you're in more of a sit-down mood, try the **Wolfgang Puck Grand Café** (tel. 714/634–9653) or **Johnny Rockets** (tel. 714/769–4500).

VENICE BEACH

4

I f you're looking for a beach scene as opposed to just a beach, nothing beats the spectacle that is Venice Beach.

This diverse sand-side habitat is practically a monument to funkiness, with sunbathing coming in a distant second to the featured attraction: people-watching. This is a character mecca, a perpetual parade of pedestrians, bikers, and rollerbladers all marching to the off-beat. Street performers, too, are the rage. On any given day, a stroll along Venice's paved walkway can get you front-row seats before many varied demonstrations of skill, including—but certainly not limited to—impressionists, hip-hop dancers, and chain-saw jugglers. You can marvel from the sand or pull up a chair at any of the beach-side cafés that provide the perfect venue from which to watch the show unfold.

Venice is also home to that famed outdoor palace of physical fitness, Muscle Beach, where rippling Arnold Schwarzenegger wannabes (legend has it that the Terminator was discovered

KEEP IN MIND Parking, particularly in summer, can be a bear. Arrive early to get the best spot. Lots west of Lincoln, between north and south Venice boulevards, have free shuttles running to and from the beach. Venice is definitely a daytime activity. Prepare yourself for some unseemliness (it's better territory for sexologists than for young children) and some conversation afterwards. On the other hand, a little family communication isn't so bad, and the biking and skating are great. To learn the whole cool truth about the city, take a tour with the Venice Historical Society (tel. 310/967–5170). Tours (holidays only) cost $15.

here) pump themselves up inside a chained-off area while a field of onlookers gawk from the other side. Real people get their exercise up and down the paved walkway that runs for a few miles along the beach. You can bring your own rollerblades or bikes or rent them at one of the nearby shops. If you do opt to do this, however, be prepared to have plenty of company as the Venice Boardwalk—recently resurfaced for your rolling pleasure—is one of the busiest thoroughfares around.

As for retail, there's good news and bad news. The good news is that there are plenty of funky shops peddling sunglasses, beach paraphernalia, tarot-card readings, and more. The bad news, however, is that you may have to steer your teenager away from those proprietors hawking body piercings and tattoos (maybe you can compromise and persuade her to go for a temporary tattoo). Hey, we're talking Venice here!

EATS FOR KIDS
The **Sidewalk Cafe** (1401 Ocean Front Walk, tel. 310/399-5547) has standard favorites right on the beach. The **Rose Café** (220 Rose Ave., tel. 310/399-0711) offers indoor or outdoor seating and everything from swordfish to pizza.

HEY, KIDS! Venice was created in 1905 by Abbot Kinney, a tobacco magnate from New Jersey. Local myth has it that Kinney wanted to re-create his favorite Italian city. In reality, creating canals was just the easiest way to drain the marshland. Colorful residents arrived early on. One was Jake Cox, who, in 1914, used to attract folks to his indoor pool by dressing in a fuzzy suit and setting himself on fire.

WARNER BROS. STUDIOS TOUR

One of the lures of Hollywood is that you never know whom you're going to run into, and many people are drawn to this studio tour for just that reason. Though star encounters certainly happen here, they are the exception, not the rule. You'll probably have to content yourself with a look at movie-studio magic—pretty thrilling in and of itself—and the knowledge that a celebrity—Noah Wyle, perhaps—could be somewhere in the vicinity.

Those familiar with the theme-park variety of back-lot tour (such as at Universal Studios Hollywood) may be pleasantly surprised here. This is the real (or perhaps reel) thing—more intimate and less schtick-laden and therefore more appropriate for older kids. You tour in intimate groups via golf carts, rolling through the lot while knowledgeable guides spin tales of studio legend and lore. Every tour is different, with what you see dependent

EATS FOR KIDS Universal Studios CityWalk features the **Wolfgang Puck Café** (1000 Universal Center Dr., Universal City, tel. 818/985–9653), serving the famous chef's brand of California cuisine. People in the "biz" are rumored to like **Dalt's** (3500 W. Olive Ave., tel. 818/953–7750), a hospitable American grill.

KEEP IN MIND Guidelines allow children 8 and up, but the education-oriented fare is best for those a bit older. The roughly 2¼-hour tours require walking, so wear good shoes. Though tours operate year-round, encountering work in progress is less likely during hiatus periods around Christmas and in late spring/early summer. Reservations are required, but last-minute visitors can occasionally be accommodated. Also try the Paramount Studios Tour (5555 Melrose Ave., tel. 323/956–1777) or the shorter (70 minutes) tour given by NBC (3000 W. Alameda Ave., tel. 818/840–3537).

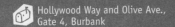
Hollywood Way and Olive Ave.,
Gate 4, Burbank

$32

818/954–1744;
wbsf.warnerbros.com/cmp/addition.htm

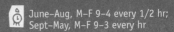
June–Aug, M–F 9–4 every 1/2 hr;
Sept–May, M–F 9–3 every hr

10 and up

upon what's filming and what areas are open that day. In fact, some people take the tour several times. A typical day might include a trip through the wardrobe department, followed by some photo ops in front of the trolley diner featured on *ER*. (Only still cameras are allowed, and photography may be limited.) A fun stop—if it's not in use for a production—is the studio's Old West town set, where you can look for the blind school from *Little House on the Prairie* as well as the saloon familiar from such Westerns as *Maverick*.

True movie aficionados will no doubt be in heaven here, but even non-movie buffs are bound to be delighted. Yes, thousands take the tour each year, but you will nevertheless feel like you're getting VIP treatment. The excursion, in fact, is actually named the VIP Tour, because it was originally created to entertain visiting dignitaries during the studio's early years.

HEY, KIDS! Complete the "insider" experience by perusing the racks at It's a Wrap! Productions (3315 W. Magnolia Blvd., tel. 818/567-7366), where you can purchase outfits last worn in your favorite TV shows and films. Half the fun is owning a piece of Hollywood; the other is getting great bargains, such as a Banana Republic shirt (perhaps worn in *Beverly Hills, 90210*) for $5. You won't find the stars' clothing (those are pricier items categorized as "collectibles"), but you'll get a conversation piece.

WILDLIFE WAYSTATION

U nder ordinary circumstances, coming face to face with a lion would be cause for panic. At the Wildlife Waystation, it's an occasion for awe. Close encounters of the wildlife kind are the hallmark of this unique facility in the Angeles National Forest. Unlike a zoo, where hundreds of feet typically separate humans and beasts, animals encountered here—about 1,100–1,200 at any one time, including lions, tigers, coyotes, primates, and bears—are only a few feet away, separated by their enclosures. That means you'll "get close enough to hear them purr," as one guest put it, and can appreciate the full size of, say, a Bengal tiger. And when all 60 lions roar, as they occasionally do, "you can hear it all throughout the canyon," says founder Martine Colette.

Such proximity can be accomplished only at a rare place like the Waystation. While zoo residents need a human comfort zone because of their daily showings, animals here receive guests only one or two days a month and by appointment only (in other words, reservations are required). The infrequent company diminishes the animals' stress level and allows them

KEEP IN MIND Call for reservations at least a week ahead—two in summer. Children younger than 5 can be accommodated, but you'll probably need to carry them, at least part of the time. This is definitely not a stroller-friendly park; terrain is rugged and unpaved. Sunday tours run roughly 70 minutes. During the summer, the Waystation offers several Saturday evening tours in darkness. These strolls occur at a time when nocturnal animals—normally lounging during the day—can be seen and, more important, heard. The price for the evening walks includes an on-site dinner but is only for visitors 16 and up.

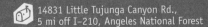
14831 Little Tujunga Canyon Rd.,
5 mi off I–210, Angeles National Forest

818/899–5201; www.waystation.org

Tour $12 ages
12 and up, $6
children 3–11

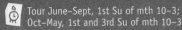
Tour June–Sept, 1st Su of mth 10–3;
Oct–May, 1st and 3rd Su of mth 10–3

5 and up

to feel comfortable up close and personal. Far from just an animal showcase, Colette's creation is a sanctuary, a place where animals come when they have nowhere else to go. Some have been abandoned, others became homeless after the closing of a circus or zoo, while still others have been rescued from inappropriate keepers who have mistreated them.

A private institution (Colette bought the 160-acre canyon spread after her traditional suburban home could no longer accommodate her "finds," such as a cougar), the Waystation is licensed by all animal authorities at the local, state, and federal levels, meaning all enclosures meet or exceed specified guidelines. Though education is paramount here, one of the other great perks is the walk through the serenely rural surroundings—only ½ hour north of downtown Los Angeles but nevertheless another part of the world.

HEY, KIDS! The Waystation gets lots of iguanas—over 100 once. Why? Folks buy them as cute babies but don't know what to do when they grow. The average baby is pocket-size but can grow to 5 feet or more. That's a lot of lizard. Thankfully, even the big guys are vegetarians.

EATS FOR KIDS Wildlife Waystation's canyon location makes it remote from many restaurants. Just a hop away, the **Ranch Side Café** (11355 Foothill Blvd., Lake View Terrace, tel.818/834–0031) has sandwiches, burgers, some Mexican fixings, and other basic American entrées. About 10 minutes away, in Sunland, you'll find numerous fast-food joints as well as a **Coco's** (10521 Sunland Blvd., tel. 818/353–5677), a diner-style eatery with sandwiches, burgers, and the like. About 15 minutes away, in Pasadena, there's much more to choose from.

WILD RIVERS WATERPARK

With some of the world's most sought-after attractions nearby, you might think that home-grown Wild Rivers just wouldn't stack up. Nothing could be further from the truth. A compact water park with a bit of neighborhood appeal, it still manages to offer about 40 attractions in total: some to cool you off, others to warm you up, and a good supply of slides that can literally thrill the swimsuit right off of you.

Prospective sliders can pretty much guess the nature of the ride by its moniker. If it's named something like the Ledge, the Edge, or the Abyss, it's a sure bet that you'll be flinging yourself down something winding, fast, and scary. Wipeout hurls you down a slide ahead of 1,000 gallons of water, while Chaos, predictably, is similarly disorienting. Bombay Blasters shoots you out like a cannonball, so hold onto your trunks. You can also float on a lazy river or choose your brand of wave-pool surf from either the gentle current of Monsoon Lagoon or the cranked-up waves of Hurricane Harbor (the latter for expert swimmers only).

EATS FOR KIDS Wild Rivers has all the basics: sandwiches, fries, and snacks at **Colonel Hawkin's;** pizza at the **Congo Cafe;** and ice cream at the **Sweet Shoppe.** The **Crazy Horse Steak House** (71 Fortune Dr., tel. 949/585–9000) is just one of the eateries at the Irvine Spectrum.

KEEP IN MIND The Hurricane Harbor wave pool is for expert swimmers 54" and taller only. You'll need a boogie board to surf, and you can rent one at the central Rental Shack for $4 per day. Lockers and inner tubes are also available for rent. Ask about discounted "Dry" passes for visitors arriving as spectators only and "Car Load" discounts, offered late June–Labor Day, Mondays 4–8. The cost is $40 per carload, up to eight; after that, it's an additional $5 per person (plus $5 for parking). Additionally, individual passes go down to $12 (ages 3 and up) after 4 PM.

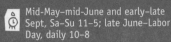
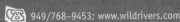

Thrills here are mercifully not (if you'll pardon the expression) over the edge. There's plenty to get wet and wild on, but preteens—even the daring ones—seem to like Wild Rivers' slides for being scary, but not too scary. Little kids like their chance to slide like the big kids (the kiddie sections have miniature versions of some of the big-people attractions), whereas parents generally laud Wild Rivers for being small enough so they can keep an eye on their youngsters at all times.

In fact, size seems to be the big bonus here. When compared to other water parks—nearby Raging Waters (*see* #17), for example, is more than twice as big—Wild Rivers is intimate. You won't feel as though you're trekking miles to get from one ride to another, and you can go home feeling like you've actually done it all. Don't think, however, that that means your kids won't want to come back. They will—repeatedly.

HEY, KIDS! The Patriot, a four-person in-line flume ride, stands seven-stories tall, the only one like it in southern California. Wonder why it's called the Patriot? The red, white, and blue flume seems to resemble a Patriot missile, and you'll feel like you're rocketing as you careen forwards and even backwards for a time. Tip: If you're on the small side, stock your boat with some bigger folks (a couple of dads wouldn't hurt). The heavier you are, the faster you'll go.

CLASSIC GAMES

"I SEE SOMETHING YOU DON'T SEE AND IT IS BLUE." Stuck for a way to get your youngsters to settle down in a museum? Sit them down on a bench in the middle of a room and play this vintage favorite. The leader gives just one clue—the color—and everybody guesses away.

"I'M GOING TO THE GROCERY..." The first player begins, "I'm going to the grocery and I'm going to buy... " and finishes the sentence with the name of an object, found in grocery stores, that begins with the letter "A." The second player repeats what the first player has said, and adds the name of another item that starts with "B." The third player repeats everything that has been said so far and adds something that begins with "C" and so on through the alphabet. Anyone who skips or misremembers an item is out (or decide up front that you'll give hints to all who need 'em). You can modify the theme depending on where you're going that day, as "I'm going to X and I'm going to see..."

FAMILY ARK Noah had his ark—here's your chance to build your own. It's easy: Just start naming animals and work your way through the alphabet, from antelope to zebra.

PLAY WHILE YOU WAIT

NOT THE GOOFY GAME Have one child name a category. (Some ideas: first names, last names, animals, countries, friends, feelings, foods, hot or cold things, clothing.) Then take turns naming things that fall into that category. You're out if you name something that doesn't belong in the category—or if you can't think of another item to name. When only one person remains, start again. Choose categories depending on where you're going or where you've been—historic topics if you've seen a historic sight, animal topics before or after the zoo, upside-down things if you've been to the circus, and so on. Make the game harder by choosing category items in A-B-C order.

DRUTHERS How do your kids really feel about things? Just ask. "Would you rather eat worms or hamburgers? Hamburgers or candy?" Choose serious and silly topics—and have fun!

BUILD A STORY "Once upon a time there lived..." Finish the sentence and ask the rest of your family, one at a time, to add another sentence or two. Bring a tape recorder along to record the narrative—and you can enjoy your creation again and again.

GOOD TIMES GALORE

WIGGLE & GIGGLE Give your kids a chance to stick out their tongues at you. Start by making a face, then have the next person imitate you and add a gesture of his own—snapping fingers, winking, clapping, sneezing, or the like. The next person mimics the first two and adds a third gesture, and so on.

JUNIOR OPERA During a designated period of time, have your kids sing everything they want to say.

THE QUIET GAME Need a good giggle—or a moment of calm to figure out your route? The driver sets a time limit and everybody must be silent. The last person to make a sound wins.

HIGH FIVES

BEST IN TOWN
Disneyland
Fort MacArthur Museum
La Brea Tar Pits and the Page Museum
Legoland
Magicopolis

BEST OUTDOORS
Paramount Ranch

WACKIEST
Bunny Museum

BEST CULTURAL ACTIVITY
Olvera Street

NEW & NOTEWORTHY
Disney's California Adventure

BEST MUSEUM
La Brea Tar Pits and the Page Museum

SOMETHING FOR EVERYONE

ALL AROUND TOWN

SAN FERNANDO VALLEY
Television Tapings, 9
Universal Studios Hollywood, 7
Warner Bros. Studios Tour, 3

SAN PEDRO
Cabrillo Marine Aquarium, 62
Fort MacArthur Museum, 49
Los Angeles Maritime Museum, 35

SANTA MONICA
Magicopolis, 33
Museum of Flying, 29
Pacific Park, 24
Puppetolio, 19

SANTA MONICA MOUNTAINS
Paramount Ranch, 22
Satwiwa, 14

VENICE
Venice Beach, 4

WESTSIDE
Getty Center, 48
Museum of Tolerance, 28

MANY THANKS

Writing this book took the help (and patience!) of some extraordinary people. My thanks go to all the Los Angeles area PR people—particularly Carol Martinez and Stacy Litz at the Los Angeles Convention and Visitors Bureau and Elaine Cali and Jennifer Gonzalez at the Anaheim Orange County Visitor & Convention Bureau—who kept answering my phone calls no matter how many hundreds of times I called. To all my L.A. friends who stuck with me as I dragged them through yet another Los Angeles attraction— I couldn't have done it without you. More thanks to my oh-so-wonderful editor, Andrea Lehman, who made the book more literate and the process more fun. To my daughters, Alexis and Melissa, who put up with way too many hours of mommy writing—I love you. And finally, to my incredible husband, Steve—without your patience, sense of humor, and late-night omelets, this book would never have happened.

—Lisa Oppenheimer

the end.